# A HISTORY *of* HOCKEY *in* CANADA

## J. Alexander Poulton

OVER
TIME
BOOKS

© 2010 by OverTime Books
First printed in 2010 10 9 8 7 6 5 4 3 2 1
Printed in Canada

The Publisher: OverTime Books is an imprint of Éditions de la Montagne Verte

Library and Archives Canada Cataloguing in Publication

Poulton, J. Alexander (Jay Alexander), 1977–
        A history of hockey in Canada / J. Alexander Poulton.

Includes bibliographical references.
ISBN 978-1-897277-56-0

        1. Hockey—History. I. Title.

GV846.5.P68 2010          796.96209          C2010-900575-9

*Project Director*: J. Alexander Poulton
*Editor*: Carla MacKay
*Cover Image*: 16 May, 1976, Philadelphia, Pennsylvania, USA— Montréal Canadiens hug and kiss the Stanley Cup following their four-game sweep of the Philadelphia Flyers during the Stanley Cup Finals at the Spectrum Sports Arena. © Bettmann/CORBIS

We acknowledge the financial support of the Government of Canada through the Book Publishing Industry Development Program (BPIDP) for our publishing activities.

Canadian Heritage     Patrimoine canadien

*PC*: 1

# Contents

Introduction . . . . . . . . . . . . . . . . . . . . . . . . . . . . . . . .5

Chapter 1:
The Hockey Family Tree . . . . . . . . . . . . . . . . . . . . .17

Chapter 2:
The Heart of the Game . . . . . . . . . . . . . . . . . . . . . .26

Chapter 3:
Tools of the Game . . . . . . . . . . . . . . . . . . . . . . . . .46

Chapter 4:
Lord Stanley of Preston and His Cup . . . . . . . . . . . .78

Chapter 5:
Women's Hockey in Canada . . . . . . . . . . . . . . . . . .104

Chapter 6:
The Minority Leagues . . . . . . . . . . . . . . . . . . . . . .119

Chapter 7:
The Enduring Canadian Franchises—A Short
History . . . . . . . . . . . . . . . . . . . . . . . . . . . . . . . . .129

Chapter 8:
Canadian Hockey's First Shrines . . . . . . . . . . . . . .205

Chapter 9:
Hockey Moves South . . . . . . . . . . . . . . . . . . . . . . .210

Chapter 10:
The Canadian Expansion . . . . . . . . . . . . . . . . . . . .225

Chapter 11:
Hockey Timeline . . . . . . . . . . . . . . . . . . . . . . . . . .243

Notes on Sources . . . . . . . . . . . . . . . . . . . . . . . . .254

# Dedication

To my mother, Candace

# Introduction

> *To spectator and player alike, hockey gives the release that strong liquor gives the repressed man. It is the counterpoint of Canadian self-restraint, it takes us back to the fiery blood of Gallic and Celtic ancestors who found themselves minorities in the cold, new environment and had to discipline themselves as all minorities must.*
>
> –Hugh MacLennan, *Two Solitudes*

How to define Canada is something Canadians are always contemplating. The country's history includes, but is not limited to, stories of explorers, French missionaries, forgotten Native tribes, federal government and multiculturalism—all parts of distinct narratives that have been stitched together to form the second largest country in the world. While other nations can look to tumultuous historical moments for excitement, like the American Civil War or the French Revolution, Canada has a somewhat less-intriguing past. Expo '67 or the passing of the Meech Lake Accord are hardly moments in Canada's history that contain the spirit and galvanizing ability of, say, Martin Luther King's "I have a dream" speech. So, what unites Canadians? One need look no further than hockey.

Of course, the fact that Canada is such a large country lends itself to some disparity between East Coasters and West Coasters, but just about anyone from BC to Newfoundland can strike up a conversation about the country's most common denominator, hockey. Some might argue this point, but what else resonates with the same power in every community and almost every home in the country? And before you say it, no, Tim Hortons doesn't count!

Before Canada was even called Canada, there was hockey. But, there is more to the sport than its simple existence. Looking back at the history of Canada, you see how hockey, in one way or another, entered the national discourse in both the country's darkest and most glorious moments. The lessons the game of hockey provides have morphed into some of Canada's most popular metaphors. Hockey is what divides

Canadians while bringing them together at the same time.

To understand this obsession with hockey, it, of course, helps to dig out the history books. But where to begin? In the late 1960s, a special commission was actually formed in Canada to solve the mystery as to where hockey was first played and to explain how it developed into the sport that North Americans enjoyed with such fervour.

Baseball went through a similar process with the establishment of the Mills Commission in 1905 that helped determine the exact origin of the game. The commission discovered the following in its final report:

> "*The best evidence obtainable to date,* [baseball] *was devised by Abner Doubleday at Cooperstown, New York, in 1839...in the years to come, in the view of the hundreds of thousands of people who are devoted to baseball, and the millions who will be, Abner Doubleday's fame will rest evenly, if not quite as much, upon the fact that he was its inventor...as upon his brilliant and distinguished career as an officer in the Federal Army.*"

However, since that report was published, historians have revealed the Abner Doubleday story is nothing more than that, a story. At the time,

Major League Baseball (MLB) seemed more interested in promoting a grand legend of its sport instead of the truth, and the idea of a famous general as the creator of America's favourite pastime was just too tempting for MLB's marketing department to pass up. The myth was used extensively to help spread the popularity of the game and to gain support for the construction of the Baseball Hall of Fame in Cooperstown in 1939.

The hockey commission wanted to avoid the same debacle and aimed to truthfully sort through all the myths and politics that surrounded the foundations of hockey, but after an exhaustive search, the commission was forced to conclude that with so many undocumented accounts lost to history, it could not so much as come up with a conclusive birthplace for hockey.

What the investigation did discover, however, was that most of the early information about hockey's beginnings was centred in and around Nova Scotia, Québec and Ontario. But without concrete evidence, it was clear to the commission and historians alike that no one community could claim to have invented hockey. As it was eventually revealed in baseball, and as is the case with most other sports, hockey did not suddenly spring into being—its development was a long process of evolution that did not start in Canada.

One of the most popular references in the history of hockey outside North America comes from the paintings of several 17th- and 18th-century Dutch artists. For example, in Hendrick Avercamp's depiction of Dutch citizens playing a game that uses skates and sticks, the connection to modern hockey is minor, but the painting clearly traces a line back to the roots of the game.

Even before the 17th century, there was the Irish game of "hurling," which has been played on the Emerald Isle for longer than its recorded history and was most likely first introduced by Celtic tribes. Traditionally a summer sport, hurling was just as easily played on ice in the wintertime. It was also known for its particularly brutal play on the field and was banned several times by the Irish clergy. People in Ireland kept playing, though, and it was hurling and its variants that soldiers in the British army brought to North America in the early 18th and 19th centuries, when the game began to influence the early development of hockey.

But where did hockey first find its foothold in Canada? Hockey author Garth Vaughan has put together an extremely convincing argument for hockey having developed out of Windsor, Nova Scotia, on a pond at King's College, but with so many other claims on where the game began, it's difficult to state unequivocally that hockey was born in this one place and this one place only.

What is clear is that once hockey got its start in Canada, word spread quickly, and Canadians embraced the new sport—even if they didn't know what it was. From about 1800 to 1874, hockey didn't really have an identity of its own. It was called "hurley-on-ice," "rickets" and, yes, hockey, but there was no rulebook to speak of. Regulations differed from city to city, even rink to rink, so what hockey needed was for the sport to come off the pond and into the arena. Doing so would put limitations on the game, force players to follow rules and, most importantly, allow players to develop their skating and puckhandling skills.

Moving indoors was the first step toward legitimizing the sport of hockey. That first indoor game occurred in Montréal on March 3, 1875. Halifax native James Creighton was looking for a way to keep his rugby teammates in shape over the long winter months, and he remembered the sport he had learned as a child on the ice in and around his hometown. Using what he knew as the rules and regulations, he spent some time teaching his friends how to play, and on March 3, they held an exhibition match at Montréal's Victoria Skating Rink. The *Montréal*

*Gazette* even reported on the game, calling it an "interesting and well-contested affair, the efforts of the players exciting much merriment." The game played that night would be hardly recognizable to most people today, but there is no doubt that it was a game of hockey destined to change the sport forever.

As hockey grew in popularity, various leagues began to spring up across Canada, but something crucial was lacking, and that something was an ultimate tournament that unified the teams in working and playing for an end goal. So, Lord Stanley of Preston, governor general of Canada from 1888 to 1893, purchased a small silver bowl that was to be awarded, at the conclusion of the hockey season, to recognize the top amateur team in the country. Originally named the Dominion Hockey Challenge Cup, what we know now as the Stanley Cup became the ultimate symbol of Canadian hockey supremacy.

When the Cup was first awarded in 1893, teams weren't overly eager to win the actual trophy because it stood just a few centimetres off the ground and had a rule attached to it that teams couldn't keep it—what was the point? But as each year passed, and the battle to be crowned Cup champion intensified, a legend and mythology began to surround the Cup. Teams went to great lengths to get the chance to win it. No other story exemplifies this determination more than that of the Dawson City Nuggets' journey in 1904–05 from the Yukon to Ottawa. The team faced nasty weather, avalanche delays, the prospect of walking some of the way to Ottawa and, not surprisingly, exhaustion, all for the hope of winning the Cup.

However, of every team looking to earn a piece of immortality by winning hockey's highest honour, without a doubt the greatest three from the early years of hockey in Canada were Ottawa, Montréal and Toronto. The Ottawa Senators were the best there was, with some of the greatest players in the history of the game gracing the team's lineup. From 1883 to the present day, the Ottawa Senators have always given their fans something to cheer for.

The Montréal Canadiens, on the other hand, got their start in 1909, and since then have had the most hockey success by any one franchise, with 24 Stanley Cup wins. Countless individual player awards, some of the best rosters ever and a fan base that has always bordered on fanaticism haven't hurt, either.

Toronto started out with a different team name than the Maple Leafs we know today, and the power and legend this franchise holds in the history of hockey can never be diminished. Since the team's creation in 1917 when they were called the Arenas, Toronto hockey fans have celebrated 13 Stanley Cup wins and have cheered for some of the greatest hockey legends of all time.

But professional hockey couldn't remain locked up in Canada forever, and by the early 1900s, several American teams had established a presence on the rink and had even won a Stanley Cup. One of the biggest early hockey players in the United States was Hobey Baker. The suave, handsome scholar from New York City played in only 45 games in his brief hockey career, but in those games, had no trouble bringing out the sophisticated crowds of the big city. Unfortunately, Baker was killed in an accident just after World War I ended, but in no way did hockey end with him. Hockey fever had spread throughout the U.S., and teams from California to Boston began to pop up throughout all levels of hockey.

Eventually, the National Hockey League (NHL) was formed in 1917, and among many teams in the U.S., pro squads were also organized in Vancouver, Edmonton, Winnipeg and Québec City. Some were not destined to survive the business of hockey, and, as we know, the Winnipeg

Jets and Québec Nordiques now only exist in the Hockey Hall of Fame.

In addition to where hockey began and which cities had the most prominent teams, another way the history of the game is tracked is through the development of the tools needed to play hockey. Once hockey moved indoors in the late 1800s, its progress really began to speed up as the equipment became more refined. Official rules needed to be written, players' skills had to be honed and new equipment needed to be invented. In these early days, hockey equipment was borrowed, for the most part, from the sport's "parents," so to speak.

When hockey first began to develop in the early 1800s, hurleys and wooden discs, as well as horse apples (use your imagination), were the standards for sticks and pucks, and the first skate blades were made by blacksmiths. Players tied the blades to their boots using strips of cowhide, making their "skates" unstable and uncomfortable. Skate technology eventually improved, and, coincidentally, so did the players. But as the pace of the game increased, the players, and the goalies especially, needed sturdier skates and better body protection because shots were coming harder and bruises were getting bigger with the advent of professional leagues in the late 19th century. When the

NHL arrived in 1917, companies looking to open up new markets refined hockey equipment even further, and the professionals put their products to good use.

Equipment in the modern NHL is now specifically tailored for the sport and to get the maximum performance from the player—a far cry from, say, skates strapped to a player's boots.

But what of the women, a facet of hockey that is quite prominent now? Truthfully, it's a story that often gets left out of hockey history, but from the beginning, women were standing right beside their male counterparts, eager to learn and develop the sport. Lady Isobel Stanley, daughter of Lord Stanley, played hockey with her brothers on Canada's first-ever backyard rink at Rideau Hall, and, in 1890, she organized one of the first women's games on record.

Despite Lady Isobel's zeal for women's participation in hockey, there was a marked difference in how the sexes played the game. While men took to the ice free from societal constraints, women were expected to abide by certain rules of femininity. From the 1890s to the 1920s, the standard uniform of a female hockey player was a thick, heavy sweater, a large toque and an ankle-length skirt made of cumbersome fabric. No, it wasn't easy, but the women persevered, and eventually, rules were relaxed, and women's hockey began to gain the respect it deserved. This was not something that occurred over a decade— every generation since Lady Isobel has battled to earn a place in the traditionally male-dominated sport. Women's hockey has come a long way, though, and Canadians like Hayley Wickenheiser and Manon Rheaume have created a buzz around the game that, up until now, had never been experienced by "the fairer sex." Canada's women's national team is considered the best in the world and, because of their skill and dedication, the legion of fans interested in their brand of hockey continues to grow as each season passes.

Other countries besides Canada and the U.S. have now embraced hockey—both for men and women—but the following chapters show that this sport could not have developed into what it is today without Canada. It was in Canada that the sport emerged, the rules were written, the leagues were organized, the Stanley Cup was born and hockey became a way of life.

# Chapter 1

# The Hockey Family Tree

Figuring out the origins of hockey is not as simple as pointing to a place and time of creation and saying it is so. Sure, there would be little argument if you said hockey is a Canadian game and it has become what it is because of Canadian involvement. But, like any historical timeline, family tree or genealogical chart, there are foreign roots, and in hockey, these roots can be traced back to other sports that have undoubtedly influenced the development of the game we experience today.

## Hurling

The sport of hurling has been around since Stonehenge was first constructed in 2500 BC, and it remains a popular sport in its native Ireland to this day. The object of the game is simple: players use a wooden stick called a hurley to hit a small ball past an opponent's

> **QUICK FACT:** A hurley in Gaelic is called a *camán*.

netminder who is positioned between two goal-posts. Play is extremely fast, and a great amount of individual skill is required to compete at the professional level. One of the biggest similarities between modern-day hockey and hurling is the physicality of both sports. Body checking is allowed in hockey and in hurling, and players are no strangers to bench brawls.

Hurling, however, is played on a field, and when Irish immigrants arrived in Canada in the late 1700s, they discovered seasons that prevented play for about half the year. Winter was the problem... but also the solution. As a remedy, the Irish put on a few extra layers and took their game to the ice. It's likely they thought to try this because they had seen Natives also playing games on the ice. After all, when life hands you ice, make...ice?

It didn't take long for hurling to evolve because the ice necessitated the adaptation of skates, the reinvention of the hurley and a rethinking of the rules. Soon, "hurley-on-ice" looked nothing like the sport originally brought over from the old country. Hurling came to resemble more and more an early form of hockey.

**QUICK FACT:** As the game of hurling was redeveloped, it came to be known by many different names: break-shins, wicket and rickets, to name a few.

## Bandy

The game of bandy was one of the first stick-and-ball games played on ice and, like hurling, is played today and still resembles hockey in many ways. The most obvious similarities are the speed and physical nature of the sports. Bandy also likely had an influence on the development of hockey because it took existing, similar games like hurling and cricket and brought them onto the ice.

Games similar to bandy have been written about in Russian monastery records as early as the 10th century, but the sport itself seemed to have become popularized in the early 1700s. Russians consider themselves the creators of bandy, which is no surprise considering "bandy" in Russian means "Russian hockey." Also during the 18th century, but in the east in Wales, a game similar to bandy was being played and was named "bando." Its earliest mention is found in a 1770 Welsh dictionary by John Walters.

The British eventually took to the game, and the earliest record of a bandy/bando club is from 1813 in Bury Fen. At this time, the fens (waterways) of East Anglia froze in the winter, giving rise to a lively culture of distance skating and, of course, bandy. In 1853, even the royal family got involved when a game called "hockey on the ice" was played at Windsor Castle with Prince Albert in goal.

In a game of bandy, players attempt to move the ball toward the opponent's net by stick-handling or passing the ball to teammates. Along the way, opposing players can intercept a pass or check their opponents. This, however, is where bandy's similarities with hockey end.

The game's rules are actually more similar to soccer than those of hockey. Bandy is played on a sheet of ice the size of a soccer field, and games are split into two 45-minute halves. Two teams of 11 players each align themselves on the ice, with forwards, midfielders and defenders deciding the play of the ball. Offside and ball-in-play and out-of-play rules follow those of soccer as well.

## Shinty

Sharing an ancestry with hurling and bandy, shinty is a team sport that was mostly played in Scotland. Similar in some ways to field hockey, shinty allows far more physical contact in the course of a game than what is acceptable in hurling or bandy.

A direct cousin of hurling, shinty grew into its own sport in the Scottish Highlands. Its exact origins are impossible to decipher, but it is known that shinty has been played in Scotland for at least 2000 years. The shinty ball was originally made of wood or bone, but was later made from tough leather, and it's believed the name "shinty" comes from the cries uttered during the game and the physical, almost violent, nature of the sport. In fact, in Scotland, it wasn't uncommon for shinty games to be targets for government and church officials because matches often led to bouts of drinking and brutishness.

> **QUICK FACT:** "Shinty" means commotion or brawl.

The Scots traditionally played shinty throughout the entire year. The most popular time to partake in the game, however, was on New Year's Day when entire villages gathered and played in one large match. When the game was brought to Canada in the early 1800s, many Scottish immigrants continued to play it, but over time, the sport evolved in the different climate and became mixed with other sports like bandy and hurling.

There are two things about shinty that are instrumental when considering the development of hockey. In shinty, players are allowed to hit the ball with both sides of their sticks, and a player can also hit the ball while it is in the air. These two particular rules are important because they were incorporated into early games of hockey in Canada when Scottish immigrants brought shinty to the country. And now, as most hockey fans know,

> **QUICK FACT:** Not taking too much of a leap, the term "shinny" hockey comes from the name "shinty."

players can work the puck with both sides of their sticks and are allowed to knock the puck out of the air, as long as it is hit below the level of the crossbar.

## Mi'kmaq Ice Game: Oochamkunutk

When the last Ice Age retreated over Atlantic Canada, it left the landscape scarred, with thousands of lakes, ponds and rivers scattered about. This natural phenomenon created the perfect hunting and fishing grounds for the Native tribes that eventually settled on the lands. Residing in what is now Nova Scotia, the Mi'kmaq lived off the land for 10,000 years before the arrival of the first Europeans.

The abundance of water bodies in the area provided the Mi'kmaq with a constant supply of fish, and the expansive, dense land was ideal for hunting animals. But when the bitter cold of winter swept across the land and froze the lakes, ponds and rivers, fishing was a little harder. The Mi'kmaq, however, had a creative way of taking advantage of the frozen water for recreational purposes—they played a game for amusement that was strikingly similar to hockey. This game was called *oochamkunutk*.

Even though the exact details of the game have been lost to history, it's believed that two teams of no more than 10 men each took to the ice with sticks fashioned out of a single piece of wood and then attempted to shoot a wooden or stone disc past the opponent's goalposts. The Mi'kmaq did not use skates, but because their game was similar to hockey and existed in the same geographical region where, it's argued, hockey came into being, *oochamkunutk* deserves to be included as member of hockey's earliest influences.

Hurling. Bandy. Shinty. *Oochamkunutk*. Each their own sport, each part of how hockey in Canada developed. The similarities between these four games are obvious, and as more about the history of hockey is revealed, the initial influences they provided become all the more apparent.

## The Word "Hockey"

Hockey, as outlined by the Society for International Hockey Research, is "a game played on an ice rink in which two opposing teams of skaters, using curved sticks, try to drive a small disc, ball or block into or through the opposite goals." This is how we define the word now—but what did "hockey" mean hundreds of years ago?

"Hockey" has been part of the English language for centuries, and according to historians, derivations of the word have been found in texts from as far back as the Middle Ages. For example, "hockcarts" were two-wheeled, horse-drawn carts from the Middle Ages that were used to transport field crops. Further, there is reference to a game called hockey that farm boys of the time played covered in mud, but it obviously has nothing to do with the game of today.

**QUICK FACT:** The *Dictionary of American Slang and Colloquial Expressions* defines "hockey," or "hocky," as another word for dung, meaning, "Watch out for that hockey there in the gutter!"

One of the earliest written references to hockey, in relation to the actual sport, is from an Irish document from 1527 called the *Galway Statutes*, and it says, "The horlinge of the litill balle with hockie stickes or staves." It's likely the term "hockie" was first used in relation to the "stickes" because hurling sticks were called "hurleys" or, more recognizably, hockeys.

**QUICK FACT:** The French were also known to use a word similar to hockey long ago. An *hoquet* was a shepherd's crook, as well as a game similar to that of field hockey.

With all these similar-sounding words being used together—yet separately—it's easy to get confused, but setting origins aside for a moment, know this: hurley-on-ice and hockey were interchangeable words used to describe the sport until the late 1800s when "hockey" finally took over as the one and only name for, well, hockey.

# Chapter 2

# The Heart of the Game

Hockey might have evolved from sports first played outside of North America, but there is little doubt that hockey, as we now know it, first took shape in Canada. The soul of hockey is here, and Canadians nurtured the sport from an early age, spreading its practice from the frozen ponds of Nova Scotia to the rinks of BC. And it was during hockey's formative years, from 1893 to 1945, that it was fully and rapidly embraced by all levels of society in Canada and became the sport of the nation.

The Hockey Hall of Fame, in Toronto, Ontario, recognizes five official locales that have a legitimate claim to being the birthplace of hockey in Canada. These places are Kingston, Ontario; Deline, Northwest Territories; Windsor, Nova Scotia; the Halifax region in Nova Scotia; and Montréal, Québec. While these regions are what researchers have settled on today, there was once a push to proclaim a single birthplace for hockey in Canada in the early 1940s when plans for a hockey hall of fame began. Newspapers from hockey's major hubs suggested the natural home for a hockey hall of fame was in the birthplace of the sport, but this turned out to be so difficult to declare that arguments about the topic continue to this day. One of the first cities to stand up and proclaim itself the birthplace of hockey, however, was Kingston, Ontario, in the 1940s.

## Kingston's Sutherland Claim

Captain James T. Sutherland was a man with a huge passion for hockey, and he spent most of his life servicing the advancement of the sport in Canada. The list of his accomplishments in the hockey world is so long that he is often called the "Father of Hockey."

Born in Kingston, Ontario, in 1870, Sutherland was a devotee of the sport from an early age, and he played organized hockey on a regular basis until the age of 17. Giving up his pursuit of the game because he thought he couldn't compete, Sutherland concentrated his energy behind the scenes and was a major influence on the sport. He coached local teams and organized men's hockey leagues; in 1910, he was made a member of the Ontario Hockey Association (OHA), and by

1915 he was the association's president. During his time at the helm of the OHA, he helped organize the Frontenac Hockey Club of Kingston, and he introduced a rule change whereby the positions of point and cover point were altered to those of right and left defence.

During World War I, Sutherland had a loud voice for the young men who fought and died for Canada, and because of them, he created a trophy in their honour—the Memorial Cup, the symbol of ultimate victory in Canadian junior hockey. Sutherland's passion for hockey and his allegiance to British military ideals were so strong that he often equated the two, encouraging young men to take up arms and play the greatest game of their lives. When World War I ended, Sutherland's support of the military and hockey continued. In 1923, he helped to establish the annual hockey match between the Royal Military College of Canada and the United States Military Academy at West Point, an event that still happens today.

There was no doubt about Sutherland's place in the upper echelon of hockey's official development in Canada, so when the search for a city in which to build a hockey hall of fame began in the early 1940s, he was one of the first to stand up and proclaim his native city of Kingston as the birthplace of hockey. He based his argument on a report of a series of games between the students of the Royal Military College and Queen's University in 1888. Sutherland claimed this first actual organized game on record took place in front of Kingston's city hall. But he unwittingly contradicted himself in his story, saying the players had borrowed sticks from an "eastern firm." Well, what were these eastern firms using these sticks for, if not hockey? Despite this reason to give pause to Sutherland's argument, he was so well respected in the local hockey community that no one openly challenged his authority on the subject. However, his claim had a couple other holes as well. The game Sutherland claimed was played in Kingston between the Royal Military College and Queen's University actually took place in 1886, not 1888. And with regards to that first organized game of hockey, evidence overwhelmingly points away from Kingston and instead to Montréal, where on March 3, 1875, a game was played at the Victoria Skating Rink.

Quick to dismiss that game in 1875, staid defenders of Kingston as the birthplace of hockey like to point to an even earlier source that they see as evidence in their favour. British officer Sir Arthur Henry Freeling, who was stationed in Kingston, made an entry in his diary in January 1843, noting, "Began to skate this year, improved quickly and had great fun at hockey on the ice." This small sentence sealed the deal for Kingston's hockey enthusiasts, but a researcher at the Society for International Hockey Research later came across a letter written by Sir John Franklin in 1825 that made reference to hockey being played on the frozen waters of Great Bear Lake in the Northwest Territories. Franklin's letter states, "...the game of hockey played on the ice was the morning's sport." This simple line directly refuted Sutherland's claims and added another city to the great hockey birthplace debate.

## The Northwest Territories' Claim

"Hockey" was once the word used to describe a variety of sports that looked nothing like the game as it is today, and this created a problem with many of the early claims of this town or that town as the birthplace of hockey. What was "hockey" to these people? In the beginning, no one had a concrete definition. This is the hitch when looking into the declaration by Deline (formerly Fort Franklin), Northwest Territories, that it is the home of hockey.

On an expedition in 1825 to discover a clear passage from Europe to Asia, English explorer

Sir John Franklin dropped anchor for the winter near the shores of Great Bear Lake in the Northwest Territories. It was during this time that he wrote in a letter to Roderick Murchison, dated November 6, 1825, "Till the snow fell the game of hockey played on the ice was the morning's sport."

This is as far as Franklin's reference to the playing of hockey goes. Were the players using skates or a puck? Was he referring to field hockey played on ice? Or something else entirely that simply used a derivation of the word "hockey"? It's impossible to know, so despite Deline's claims to be the birthplace of hockey, the evidence it presents just seems too circumstantial.

## Hockey's Home Province

Ontario. The Northwest Territories. Sure, they have their advocates and claims, but the fact remains that overwhelming evidence suggests hockey truly began to first take shape as an official sport in Nova Scotia. The other communities' contentions for the title of the birthplace of hockey pale in comparison to the amount of anecdotal and physical evidence that firmly place ground zero for hockey in "Canada's Ocean Playground."

The landscape of Nova Scotia provided the perfect outdoor arena for winter sports. Dotted with thousands of lakes, ponds and rivers, the province was just calling for the beginning of the good old hockey game. The fertile land of Nova Scotia and the natural harbour in Halifax both helped hockey's cause. Nova Scotia could support a large population because of its agriculture, and the harbour was prime real estate for commercial and military interests. With the expansion of Nova Scotia's settlement in the 1700s came an influx of thousands of immigrants from all over Europe who had to adapt to their new environment. In addition to adjusting economically and socially, the new arrivals had to change their sporting traditions to fit into the landscape, specifically the long, cold winters. And so, the Scottish eventually introduced the game of shinty and the Irish the game of hurling.

Long before the arrival of the Europeans, though, the Mi'kmaq (as mentioned in Chapter 1) had been playing their own stick-and-ball games and had already adapted them to the climate of the region. The Mi'kmaq played their hockey-like games in fields in the summer and tweaked those same games for the ice and snow during the winter.

With the convergence of the new immigrants and the Mi'kmaq in the Windsor/Halifax area, everyone came together to play on the frozen ponds, and something resembling hockey began to emerge.

According to many hockey researchers, the epicentre for this mix of sporting cultures was Windsor's King's College. Historians base their belief squarely on the writings of Thomas Chandler Haliburton, who in 1844 wrote about a fictional account of his days as a young student at King's College:

> ...and you boys let out racin', yelpin', hollerin' and whoopin' like mad with pleasure; and the playground, and the game at bass [base] in the fields or hurley on the long pond on the ice...

Of course, it's impossible to say what was going on in Haliburton's mind when he wrote his passage about hurley. Was he accurately depicting what had occurred on the ice of the long pond? He might have reconstructed the scene from a flawed

**QUICK FACT:** Thomas Chandler Haliburton was a lawyer, politician, judge and author. His reference to "hurley on the long pond on the ice" comes from his novel *The Attaché; or Sam Slick in England.* Sam Slick is an American diplomat who travels around England with the narrator, Squire Poker. The Squire acts as Haliburton, and the reference to King's College comes when Squire Poker is telling an old friend about his days back in Nova Scotia.

memory or from a random piece of information
he picked up during his travels. Haliburton's hurley snippet dates the games taking place on the ice
in Nova Scotia to sometime around the early
1800s. The ice around Windsor and King's College
(the college was established in 1789) was a popular skating spot, so it was really only a matter of
time before the students started playing sports on
the frozen water. But who, what, why and, most
importantly, when?

Key questions to consider, yes, but taken simply,
the mere mention of hurley in this time period,
in this area, is a substantial clue that cannot be
dismissed in the effort to decipher the evolution of
hockey. In fact, "hurley" was often used to refer to
the game of hockey for decades after it was first
"discovered" in Windsor. When put together with
other evidence, Haliburton's choice to write about
hurley is an important piece in the puzzle.

According to hockey historian Garth Vaughan,
in his book *The Puck Starts Here: The Origin of
Canada's Great Winter Game Ice Hockey*, during the
early to mid-1800s, besides hurley, Nova Scotians
were trying out all sorts of ice sports. Vaughan
says it was common for members of the British
military at Windsor and Halifax to experiment
with games such as cricket and field hockey
on the ice. These accounts, however, are sparse,

and the games were played on a random basis. In order for hockey to develop, there needed to be a central location where the game's variants could be played regularly, which would in turn advance the skill of the sport.

> **QUICK FACT:** The influence of cricket on the evolution of hockey is evident in the use of the word "ricket," which is a term that defined the net and was widely used in the early days of hockey.

With the nearby military forts around Windsor, rife with soldiers looking for entertainment during their downtime, and the boys at King's College, there was ample interest in letting loose. Therefore, this central meeting point needed for organized hockey must have been King's College. Or was it?

It has been pointed out by the Society for International Hockey Research that hockey might not have originated on the long pond at King's College after all. Since many of the students came from all over Nova Scotia, they were probably playing their hockey-like games in their respective communities. The following passages clearly show that a form of hurley existed around Halifax before Haliburton's book was published, and that the game had already entered the popular culture of the early 1800s.

The *Acadian Magazine* (Halifax, January 1827) carried in its pages a poem that included the following lines: "Now at ricket with hurlies some dozens of boys/Chase the ball o'er ice, with a deafening noise."

Another reference to hurley pops up two years later on February 4, 1829, in the *Colonial Patriot* in an open letter to the editor:

> *Every idler who feels disposed to profane the Lord's day, may now secure from any consequences turn out with skates on feet, hurly in hand, and play the delectable game of break-shins without any regard to laws which were made solely for the levity of manners which prevailed in the days of Charles 1st, and which are declared by our Judges to be of no validity.*

In light of these examples, it seems fair to say that King's College was, indeed, central to the evolution of hockey as a meeting place for young players, but the existence of other, earlier references to games played on the ice of Nova Scotia are just as important in hockey's timeline.

## Nova Scotia Hockey Comes to Montréal

James George Aylwin Creighton was a lawyer, an engineer and a journalist, but he is most widely known as the "Father of Hockey," even though it is a distinction he never claimed as his own. (And, if you'll remember, proponents of the Kingston claim as the birthplace of hockey call Captain James T. Sutherland their "Father of Hockey" as well.)

Born in Halifax on June 12, 1850, Creighton grew up around sports. His home on Hollis Street was just a few metres away from Halifax Harbour that in the wintertime became the place to be for all types of winter sports. Creighton spent entire afternoons watching speed skaters carve long lines across the ice, observing young couples skating slowly by the pier and lingering especially to watch the groups of older boys whack balls about with their hurley sticks. By the time Creighton grew old enough to participate in the games, hurling was the most popular sport of the time.

Hurling gained so much popularity in Halifax that it caught the attention of the editors of the *Boston Evening Gazette*, who wrote of the craze in 1859. The reporter describes in detail a game called "ricket," which he later refers to as "hockey, as it is termed here [Halifax]." He also wrote:

> *Each ricketer is provided with a hurley and*
> *all being ready a ball is thrown into the air*
> *which is the signal to commence the play, previ-*
> *ous to which, however, a ricket [goal] is chosen*

*by each side and placed in charge of a man*
[the goaltender] *whose duty it is to prevent
the ball from passing through.*

The reporter goes on to describe the action:
"Whenever the ball is put through a ricket
a shout 'game ho!' resounds from shore to shore
and dies away in hundreds of echoes through
the hills."

The existence of and participation in hockey,
or something like it, was established, but there was
no organization around the players and their
matches. What Halifax needed was someone to for-
malize the game and give the new sport legitimacy.
The man to do that was Creighton.

After finishing his studies at King's College
and graduating with an arts degree, Creighton
worked with a Halifax engineer before moving
to Montréal in 1872, where he began work
on the construction of the Lachine Canal and
the upgrading of the Montréal harbour area.
Not satisfied with the pursuits of engineering,
Creighton enrolled in the law program at McGill
University.

A sportsman through and through, Creighton
grew up playing rugby, field hockey and ice
hockey. Once in the big city of Montréal, and
surrounded by young men equally involved in
all manner of sports, Creighton became one of

McGill's most well-known athletes. Hockey, however, was a second thought for Creighton, as rugby was his sport of choice. Over the long winters in Montréal, though, he noticed members of his rugby team, the Montréal Football Club, lost some of their stamina, and so, in searching for a way to keep his teammates in shape, Creighton suggested playing a sport he had learned back home in his youth on the ice of Halifax Harbour and at King's College.

To get out of the snow and cold winds, Creighton took his team down to Montréal's Victoria Skating Rink to teach them how to play hockey. Creighton's friends quickly caught on to the game, and after several practice sessions getting the rules and regulations worked out, Creighton thought it would be a good idea to put the team's skills to use in an actual organized game.

The Victoria Skating Rink was built in 1862 and was located just below Ste-Catherine Street between Stanley Street and Drummond Street. With 10,000 square feet of ice, it was the biggest indoor skating rink in the country, was the meeting place for the city's youthful upper crust and, at night, was lit with hundreds of gaslights that gently illuminated the 15.8-metre-high iron-beamed roof. The rink, however, was not made for hockey players—it was strictly a place for leisure skating and the occasional masked ball on ice. It was not lined with any type of glass, there were no waist-high boards to protect spectators and it didn't have grandstands on which people could sit and watch games. The Victoria Skating Rink's purpose was clear: it was for the pursuits of Montréal's socialites.

Creighton, however, knew the rink manager from his time spent as a figure-skating judge, and lucky for Creighton, the manager of the rink had also seen the rugby team practicing their new game. He agreed to let Creighton play on the Victoria's ice on Sundays, but the ice time was to be kept secret from the public because Sunday was still considered sacred by the majority of the population—one word to church officials and the games would be kaput. The clandestine practices went on for a while, but Creighton and his friends eventually grew tired of hiding and decided to finally show Montréal how this new game of hockey was played.

Because there were no set rules, hurling/hockey was played by any number of players, depending on the size of the ice surface. The ice area in the Victoria Skating Rink was limited, so Creighton divided his friends into two teams of nine players to avoid on-ice chaos. But who was going to

watch the game? Creighton turned to the
*Montréal Gazette* to get the word out. On March 3,
1875, the *Gazette* published the announcement:

> *A game of hockey will be played at the
> Victoria Skating Rink this evening between two
> nines chosen from among the members. Good
> fun may be expected, as some of the players are
> reported to be exceedingly expert at the game.*

Using a set of rules that came to be known as
the "Halifax Rules," the players took to the ice
in front of 40 or so friends, curious onlookers
and one *Gazette* reporter. There were no seats for
the spectators, so to see the game, they were
forced to stand on a small elevated platform that
circled the entire rink. The gaslights provided
some visibility, and even though the rink had
a roof to protect against wind and snow, the
players skated on natural ice, which meant
no indoor heating. To add to the spectators'
malaise, there were no boards, which necessitated a keen sense of sight in the dim lighting if
one was to avoid getting hit with the ball/puck.
The *Gazette* reporter noted:

> *Hockey is played usually with a ball, but last
> night, in order that no accident should happen,
> a flat block of wood was used, so that it should
> slide along the ice without rising, and thus going
> among the spectators to their discomfort.*

With everything in place, the players "faced" the puck and started their game just after 8:00 PM. For the next hour and a half, the players skated a bruising style of hockey that left the spectators "well satisfied." The game ended with Creighton's team winning by a final score of 2–1,

**QUICK FACT:** To "face" the puck was the early 20th-century way of saying "drop the puck to start play."

and in the next day's newspaper, the *Gazette* reporter described the event as an "interesting and well-contested affair, the efforts of the players exciting much merriment."

Two days later, however, a reporter with the *Kingston Whig-Standard* got wind of a more violent version of events that occurred after the game. The *Whig-Standard*'s description of the aftermath read:

> *A disgraceful sight took place in Montréal at the Victoria Skating Rink after a game of hockey. Shins and heads were battered, benches smashed, and the lady spectators fled in confusion.*

It seems unlikely that the *Gazette* reporter would have witnessed such things and not written about them, so what might have occurred was that by the time the news of the physical game reached Kingston, it was blown out of proportion and dramatized by the *Whig-Standard* writer to sell a few more papers.

Whatever the truth about the opposing newspaper reports, what occurred on the ice at the Victoria Skating Rink was unarguably the first instance of an organized hockey game, and until Creighton gathered his friends under the roof of the Victoria, hockey was a game playedwith vague rules, in open fields and on frozen ponds. Hockey with guidelines forced players to develop skills that wouldn't have advanced if the game had remained out in the open air.

Michael McKinley, author of *Putting a Roof on Winter: Hockey's Rise from Sport to Spectacle*, argues that hockey needed the

**QUICK FACT:** It's interesting to note that in the *Gazette* article of 1875, it said, "The game of hockey, though much in vogue on the ice in New England and other parts of the United States, is not much known here, and in consequence the game of last evening was looked forward to with great interest." The reporter does not take his comment any further, but it raises the question as to whether hockey did, indeed, get its start in Canada—the writer obviously had yet to see much of the game in Montréal. Contradictions like this reinforce the challenge historians have in finding a definite answer as to where the birthplace of hockey is really located.

constraints of the indoor rink to become more than just a boys' outdoor game. McKinley noted, "It would be indoors where hockey became a sport, gaining definition and character by the very fact of its physical confinement."

Two years after Creighton's game, another contest was held at the Victoria Skating Rink, but this time there were two separate teams (who weren't friends), referees, goal umpires and different-coloured jerseys so spectators could tell the teams apart. The game pitted the St. James Athletic Club against the Metropolitan Club, for whom Creighton was captain. This time, the *Gazette* published a full report on the game, with a goal-by-goal account and a complete description of the rules that governed play on the ice:

> *Falls were frequent, and several unavoidable blows were exchanged instead of cards, with no other unpleasant results than a few bruises and much wet clothing. But fate seemed against the St. James' men and "time" was called at 6 o'clock when the Referee decided that the St. James' men had lost the match. In point of superiority the Metropolitans had decidedly the advantage as they were more active, better skaters, and played with some show of science.*

In only two years, hockey had achieved a sort of legitimacy in the sporting world, and Montréal was at the heart of its beginning. Hockey might have been born in Nova Scotia, but it grew up in Montréal.

# Chapter 3

## Tools of the Game

### The Hockey Stick

Like the game itself, the hockey stick did not simply appear one day out of thin air. It endured a long process of development, and the stick we know today is most likely an advanced form of the stick that was used in other sports like hurling and bandy.

Until the late 1890s and early 1900s, all players, including the goalie, used the same stick, and each stick was usually carved out of a single tree branch. Hockey players in Nova Scotia discovered that the hornbeam tree stood up best to the wear and tear of the game, even though the wood was extremely heavy and made stickhandling a laborious task.

One of the earliest and most popular stick types was made by the Mi'kmaq nation, and they used the tough wood of the hornbeam tree for the stick's special crafting. The Mi'kmaq sticks were a hit with hockey players because the product was sturdy and could take the abuse thrown upon it. Eventually, the official MicMac brand of stick was born. The stick's popularity was limited to those in the know, however, and James Creighton, apparently running in the right circles, had a special order of MicMacs shipped to Montréal for that first organized hockey game in 1875.

But players during this time didn't always use hockey sticks, so what did they use if they weren't privy to the MicMac? One of the earliest existing photographs of a hockey team that shows the equipment being used by its members depicts the players wielding what looks like original Irish hurley sticks. These sticks were more rounded on the end, with a wider surface area than what modern-day fans are used to seeing. Gradually, of course, the shape of the stick evolved as the game transformed. One of the main reasons for this change was the move from the hurley ball to the flat puck. The blade of the hurley stick was flush with the ice, making it difficult to manoeuvre the puck, and since modification was necessary, players began to come out onto the ice with hurley sticks that looked more and more like the hockey sticks we see today.

Although different types of wood were used, stick technology remained pretty much the same until the creation of the laminated stick in the 1940s. The laminating process involved gluing layers of wood together, thereby creating a more flexible, lighter stick. By the 1960s, companies like Sherwood began adding synthetic compounds (fibreglass) to the layering process, which made for an even more lightweight, pliable stick. This was great for the players but bad for the goaltenders. A lighter and more flexible stick meant players could fire off a quicker release and a more powerful shot—as evidenced by Bernie "Boom Boom" Geoffrion and Bobby Hull as they began to perfect the art of the slapshot.

In the 1980s, stick manufacturers began experimenting with metal compounds and introduced the single-piece aluminum stick. These sticks were stiff and hard to manage, though, so they eventually gave way to the composite stick that most NHL players now use. The primary advantage of composite sticks is, of course, their supreme light weight and flexibility that makes shots harder and faster—the goal sought all along. However, composite sticks have the annoying habit of breaking at the wrong time. Just watch any NHL game, and you will see at least three to five players' sticks break. The ultimate stick has not yet been achieved, and companies like CCM, Easton and Koho are still experimenting with different materials, such as Kevlar and titanium, in the hopes of creating the coveted perfect stick.

## The Skate

According to anthropologists, the first people to use skates were the Finns some 5000 years ago. Primitive skates were made from animal bones, and they functioned more as gliders, helping hunters conserve energy as they crossed large, frozen lakes.

It wasn't until the introduction of the metal blade and the sharpened edge that skates as we know them were born. These first skates were simply blades that attached to a platform that was fastened to a boot by rope or leather. These were called "stock" or "block" skates and were usually made by a local blacksmith. The basic design of a sharpened metal blade on the bottom of a boot has pretty much remained the same for centuries, save for a few minor adjustments.

The Dutch were the first to pioneer this technology in the 13th century, and many paintings from that era depict people on the ice, wearing skates. Ice-skating as a leisure activity, however, really caught on in the Netherlands during the

Renaissance, and paintings of people enjoying a slow skate out on the frozen rivers and ponds were not uncommon.

Skating was mainly for pleasure when it first became popular, but it didn't take long to make its way into sports, and many other Dutch paintings from the Renaissance also show village people with hooked sticks chasing a ball. Claims have been made that these paintings depict people playing an early form of hockey, but it's more likely the game that was drawn was one similar to hurling or bandy.

Leisure skating remained the most popular use for skates for quite a few years, and the activity was only embraced in North America during the late 1700s, where skates were suddenly used all the time in the cities where hockey is said to have developed. When games like hurling, shinty and bandy were introduced, they were quickly adapted to the Canadian winter, and players began taking advantage of the already-existing skate technology to more easily get around while competing on the ice. As skating as an activity for both leisure *and* sport caught on, companies that offered customers better skate options began to form.

One of the earliest manufacturers of skates in Canada was the Starr Manufacturing Company, based in Dartmouth, Nova Scotia, and founded in 1861 by John Forbes and Thomas Bateman. In 1865, they came up with an innovation that revolutionized skating and hockey—the self-fastening spring skate. This invention allowed skaters to quickly fasten or remove the blades from their boots with the flick of a lever. Prior to this, too much time was wasted in tying block skates to boots, which made skates unstable and prone to falling off during use. The spring skate allowed the skater or hockey player to have greater control on the ice, and the blade could handle frequent changes in direction without loosening or falling off. Also, before the invention of spring skates, blades were flat and long and made specifically for leisure or distance skating. Starr recognized the need for a specific style of skate for the hockey player, so it created a blade that was shorter, with a slight curve, and that had an edge with a rounded end to allow for greater turning and stopping ability. As a result, the pace of hockey increased, becoming less defensive and therefore more exciting for spectators.

In the 1880s, Starr began to change its design and offered hockey players the option of permanently fixing the blade to the boot with tiny screws. The company sold special boots, and it was left up to the customers to attach the blades themselves.

Because of Starr's unique investment in its knowledge of the sport of hockey, the company even developed a special skate for goaltenders. In their advertisements for these skates, Starr marketed the fact that its product could be purchased with or without puck stops. The puck stop was an elevation on the upper surface of the blade that blocked the puck from passing through the space between the boot and the blade. Goaltenders in those days never fell to the ice to make a save; they instead stopped pucks with their skates, so Starr's puck-stop invention prevented many goals.

At the height of the company's production in the 1920s, Starr had offices in major cities all over the world, including London, Paris, Berlin, Oslo and Moscow—even the Boston Bruins officially endorsed Starr skates. Legendary hockey man and Bruins head coach Art Ross once stated, "Your (Starr) skates have stood the test, and they will again be part of our equipment this [1924] season."

As overall technology advanced, so did skate manufacturing. More and more companies began developing hockey skates that were attached to boots, and padding for protection from pucks was introduced in the 1930s. Companies like Bauer and CCM eventually came onto the market, completely taking over. In 1939, the skates division of the Starr Manufacturing Company closed down, marking the end of the line for the famous skates that had put Canadians on the ice for generations.

The modern skates that NHL players wear today are far different from the ones Maurice Richard, or even Bobby Orr, laced up. Up until the 1970s, most skates were primarily made of leather. Gradually, synthetic materials were introduced, and skates became lighter and offered more protection against injury. Today's boot is often moulded from synthetic materials, ballistics nylon and lightweight plastics. The move to synthetic materials in the construction of the skate made players lighter and therefore increased the speed of the game. The added protection from the hard surface also resulted in fewer injuries to the foot. Companies such as Nike and Reebok have taken the construction of the hockey skate to new dimensions with the introduction of technology normally used for running shoes, like the Reebok pump in which the wearer can inject air into the boot to create a tighter fit, or Nike's air-cushioning system that creates more comfort in the sole of the boot.

In addition to being high-tech, the mark of an enviable skate is also about how good it looks. For example, some NHL players, like Alexander Ovechkin, wear skates with colourful laces and designs. But despite the packaging and the materials, a good pair of skates does not a hockey player make. True, the modern skate is lighter and offers more protection, but skates don't score goals. The best weapon a player can often have is his brain, and that, too, needs protection.

## The Helmet

Helmets in early 20th-century sports weren't used a lot, a practice that seems unimaginable today. The hockey helmet got its start (or tried to) when hockey player Barney Stanley presented a prototype to the NHL's board of governors at their annual meeting in 1927. At the time, no NHL or professional player had ever worn a hockey helmet, and Stanley's idea was quickly rejected. One year later, Boston Bruins defence-man George Owen wore a leather helmet similar to the one then used in football, but the head protection didn't catch on, and any mention of the helmet disappeared from the NHL for several years. It wasn't until an infamous incident in 1933 that the hockey helmet reappeared.

During a game that year, the Toronto Maple Leafs' star forward, Ace Bailey, suffered a horrific head injury after a vicious check from the Bruins' Eddie Shore sent Bailey crashing to the ice. Shore also suffered severe head trauma from the accident, and while Shore was able to play afterward, Bailey never stepped on NHL ice again. Boston head coach Art Ross began experimenting with helmet designs after the incident, and when he settled on one, he made his players wear the helmets in a game against the Ottawa Senators during the 1932–33 season. The following game, however, all the players, except Shore, hit the ice without their helmets, dismissing them as unnecessary and unmanly. Later on, even after Gordie Howe nearly died in March 1950 as a result of smacking his head on the ice during a game, and the Minnesota North Stars' Bill Masterton died in 1968 because of a hockey-related head injury, helmets were not made mandatory, or even widely used, in the NHL.

It wasn't until 1979 that John Ziegler, then president of the NHL, announced that the wearing of helmets was to become compulsory. The only exception to this rule was that players who had signed pro contracts prior to June 1, 1979, were exempt and the choice was theirs. At first there were a few holdouts, but helmets eventually became a permanent fixture on the ice. The final

NHL player to not wear a helmet was the St. Louis Blues' Craig MacTavish, who went helmet-less for the last time in 1997.

The hockey helmets of today still look much the same as the ones that became mandatory in 1979, but with a few differences. Rather than the previous plastic moulds, lighter and more durable synthetic materials are now used in helmets, and players have the option to attach visors to protect their eyes from errant sticks and pucks.

## The Puck

Long before the invention of the vulcanized rubber puck, all kinds of objects were smacked around in the name of hockey. As hockey grew in popularity across Canada, players could not simply go to their local sports store and pick up a puck for a few dollars (or cents, as the case might have been). Instead, they were forced to improvise with all kinds of things, from wooden discs to frozen horse droppings, affectionately known as "horse apples." Suffice it to say that horse apples were rarely used because they had a tendency to come apart in players' faces when slapped too hard.

The most common early form of the puck was the wooden disc. Usually cut from local hardwood, the wooden puck always put in a noble effort, but it could never withstand the long-term abuse players inflicted on it, and it was too light to get off any good shots. As the game grew, so too did the need for a different "disc" that could handle the kind of play that was evolving as teams began to form and leagues started to sprout in the late 1800s.

Players found the most adequate substitute for the traditional wooden disc was a rubber lacrosse ball. It had the necessary weight that allowed players to take proper shots, and it could withstand repeated hacking from the players' hockey sticks. There was just one drawback: it bounced around like a SuperBall. As you can imagine, this was especially problematic when hockey moved indoors.

Montréal's Victoria Skating Rink was the premier indoor arena of the day; it was the centre of the city's social and sporting life during the winter months, and during the 1860s, large, beautiful windows were installed to allow in as much natural light as possible. The windows were wonderful esthetically, but in combination with the lacrosse ball, they held plenty of opportunity for disaster. During one especially heated game, the players whacked at the ball with little care for any of the windows close by. Some wooden boards had been set up to protect the onlookers, but it was almost impossible to control the bouncing ball. It was only a matter of time before it cleared the boards and smashed through the arena's windows. After this occurred several times, a frustrated rink manager grabbed the ball, took a sharp knife and cut off the top and bottom sections, leaving only the flat middle piece. At first, the players were annoyed that their ball had been cut up, but then they noticed the new flat disc slid along the ice easily, still provided the resistance they needed, and most importantly, didn't smash any more windows.

When rubber pucks were invented in 1872, players didn't like them. The pucks became hard as rocks when on the ice, and when they were hit by a particularly hearty shot or struck the goalposts, they often split apart. This happened because the pucks were not made from a single piece of rubber, but laminated with a series of layers. In one famous incident during the 1902 Stanley Cup, Chummy Hill of the Toronto Wellingtons shot the puck into one of the goalposts and the puck split in two, with half flying off into a corner of

**QUICK FACT:** In the definition for "puck" in the *Canadian Oxford Dictionary*, it's noted that the word might have come from a 19th-century verb meaning "a stroke at the ball in hurling."

the rink and the other half ending up in the Winnipeg Victorias' net. Amazingly, the referee allowed the goal to stand, much to the chagrin of the Victorias.

The puck-splitting problem was later resolved with the invention of the vulcanized rubber puck, which came in one solid piece. This was the accepted construction of the puck for many years, but in the early 1990s, Fox television network decided to mess with perfection and invent the "glow puck."

Officially called the FoxTrax puck, this piece of hockey equipment was a regular puck that had a tiny computer chip inserted in the centre. The sensors inside relayed information back to the cameras that then translated the puck's movement into a bluish glow onscreen. When a player slapped the puck, a blue-hued comet tail lit up on the screen to indicate the puck's direction. And, if the puck was hit really hard, the comet tail turned red. This was all for the benefit of American viewing audiences who had complained the regular black puck was difficult to follow on the ice. The glow puck lasted until 1998 and has not been brought into the arena since. This much-maligned puck was only used on Fox, but it received so much negative press that it was eventually pulled. Lesson: don't mess with a good thing.

## Goalie Equipment
### Pads

In the early days of hockey, save for a little extra padding around the shins and chest, goaltenders didn't have any special equipment to protect themselves from the puck. Players weren't allowed to lift the puck off the ice to score a goal, so goalie equipment wasn't seen as overly necessary. It was inevitable, however, that the odd puck was going to rise off the ice and smack the goaltender right in the shinbone. Where do you think one of hockey's first names, break-shins, came from? Goaltenders eventually had enough and began to pad their most vulnerable areas, but it wasn't until one creative player decided to try something different that goalie equipment changed for good.

Before the February 16, 1896, Stanley Cup match between the Montréal Victorias and the Winnipeg Victorias, Winnipeg goaltender George "Whitey" Merritt decided to change into some new equipment. The hundreds of fans gathered to watch the game were shocked to see that Merritt was wearing a pair of cricket pads to protect his legs. There are pictures prior to 1896 that show other goaltenders wearing cricket pads, but Merritt gets credit for the invention in hockey because he wore them in a game that was considered official.

Cricket pads were widely available, so goalies made the pads work for their purposes, stuffing the insides with cotton or wool to make the pads wider and more resistant to hard shots. This worked well for a while, but as the speed of the game picked up and shots became tougher, goaltenders realized they needed more than simple pads that only covered their legs.

The first goalie pads designed specifically for hockey appeared in 1912 when the Eaton's catalogue began selling them for $4.50 per pair. These wider pads, stuffed with a variety of materials and covered in tough leather, were almost instantly popular with goaltenders. From there, not much changed in goalie-pad technology until the 1986–87 NHL season, when Boston Bruins goaltender Réjean Lemelin debuted the much lighter Aeroflex brand of pads. The synthetic material used in manufacturing the Aeroflexes made them one-third lighter than the traditional leather pads. Since the introduction of Aeroflex pads, goaltenders have dropped heavy leather pads completely, and the lightweight synthetics are standard issue from the pros down to the PeeWee leagues.

## The Trapper Glove

In the early days of hockey when men played for no other reason than a simple love of the game, goaltenders dressed similar to forwards. The only difference was that goalies wore extra padding around the chest and legs. Because their faces were exposed, pioneering goaltenders had to rely on quick reflexes and an instinct for the game in order to avoid injury. The modern goaltender now has all kinds of padding to protect him from the puck, but in the beginning, goalies didn't even have a blocker or a trapper.

A goaltender's gloves were also almost identical to those of a forward or defenceman. Some goalies modified their gloves by adding extra padding, but the objective was protection, not catching pucks. There was little advancement beyond this until 1947 when Chicago Blackhawks Emile "The Cat" Francis altered the goalie's game forever.

Francis knew the traditional-style gloves he wore game in and game out just weren't cutting it, so he began experimenting in practice with a specially designed first-baseman's mitt that had an extended protective wrapping on the wrist. After a few adjustments, Francis decided to try his new glove in a real game.

He used the glove—called a trapper—for the first time in a game against the Detroit Red Wings. But when Detroit head coach Jack Adams saw Francis' new equipment, he immediately protested to officials that the glove belonged on the baseball diamond and not in a game of hockey. Francis was allowed to wear his glove for the rest of the game, but the issue was later brought before NHL president Clarence Campbell. After some consideration, he approved the new innovation, and it was written into the rulebook that a goaltender could use a glove to "trap" the puck.

After successfully using a modified baseball glove for the trapper, Francis switched his focus to his stick hand. Tired of taking shots off this hand and having them deflect into the net because of the small surface area of impact, Francis began taping a rectangular piece of sponge rubber to the outside of his stick hand, thus inventing what eventually became the modern-day "blocker."

## The Goalie Mask

Clint Benedict was the first NHL player to wear a mask in the net, and Jacques Plante was the first to institutionalize it, but it's well known that goaltenders were seeking face protection long before these two players. Elizabeth Graham, the net protector for the women's hockey team at

Queen's University during the 1927 season, is the first person officially documented to have worn a mask for protection against injury in a game of hockey. Guarding the net for Queen's Golden Gaels, Graham wanted to shield herself from flying sticks and pucks, so she grabbed a fencing mask from the team's locker room. Little did she know what was to come from her natural instinct to protect her face and teeth. It wasn't until three years later, however, that the goalie mask made its first appearance in the NHL.

**Clint Benedict's Leather Creation.** On January 7, 1930, the Montréal Maroons were playing their local rivals, the Montréal Canadiens, in a particularly heated game. The Canadiens' star player was the legendary Howie Morenz, and all night he had been buzzing up and down the ice, giving Maroons goaltender Clint Benedict a hard time. Veteran that he was, Benedict was up to the task and made several spectacular saves to keep the score close. But then, sometime in the third period, Morenz let a vicious slapshot go from the top of the circle. The shot found its way to Benedict's face, breaking his nose and a cheekbone.

Benedict had already suffered multiple breaks to his nose this way, so after this incident, he decided to fashion a crude leather face mask to protect himself in case he got another shot in the face. Starting at his brow line, Benedict's padded mask covered his nose and the lower portion of his face, with a hole cut out for his mouth so he could breathe. In the only known picture of the mask, Benedict looks like Anthony Hopkins' Hannibal Lecter in *Silence of the Lambs*. Unfortunately, Benedict's mask didn't protect him completely, and after he took yet another shot to the face, breaking his nose once more, he was forced to retire from hockey at the end of the 1930–31 season for fear of sustaining permanent damage. After Benedict hung up his pads, no goalie donned a mask in the NHL until Jacques Plante came along, and in 1959, changed everything for good.

**The Man in the Mask.** Goaltenders were made of tough stuff in the early decades of the NHL, before the introduction of the mask and all the extra padding. Goalies often played every game of the season and did not have a backup to replace them if they were injured or having a bad game. They had to contend with players crashing into the net, sticks catching them in the face and pucks whizzing past their heads. Not wearing a mask forced goaltenders into an upright style of goaltending, and only the bravest of goalies crouched low and risked their faces by putting them directly in the line of fire. Terry Sawchuk, for example, was one of these low-crouching goaltenders. His post-NHL face clearly displayed the price he paid for being in net—he had visible scars from more than 400 stitches received during his career.

It was considered a sign of weakness for a goaltender to wear a mask, but after suffering through too many injuries, Montréal Canadien Jacques Plante often wore one during practice. He had made his own mask out of composite materials, but his coach, Toe Blake, who didn't really get along with the eccentric Plante, forbade him to wear it during a regular game for fear Plante would be thought of as puck-shy. "If you wear it when the season starts and have a bad game, the fans will blame the mask and get on you," counselled Blake.

Plante had many reasons for insisting he be allowed to wear a mask. In 1954, his right cheekbone was fractured during practice by a shot from teammate Bert Olmstead, sidelining Plante for five weeks. In 1955, Don Marshall took out Plante for five more weeks by breaking his nose and left cheekbone during practice. Said Plante in Andy O'Brien's *The Jacques Plante Story*: "I kept it [the mask] on religiously in practices from then on, wondering all the while about what kind of a mask would be practical for wearing in games."

It wasn't until 1958 that Bill Burchmore, a salesman from Fiberglass Canada Limited, approached Plante with a design that moulded to his face and allowed him to see without obstruction. The product was thin, padded and tough as steel. It actually looked kind of scary as two eyes peered out through the small holes in the mask. Coach Blake wasn't about to budge, however, and he didn't allow his goaltender to wear the new mask during games. Blake said he feared Plante wouldn't be able to see the puck or follow the plays properly. On November 1, 1959, Blake was forced to change his mind.

The Canadiens were playing the New York Rangers, and just few minutes into the first period, Rangers forward Andy Bathgate broke in from the left wing, got within five metres of the net and took a hard, rising shot that hit Plante right in the nose. The referee saw Plante go down and whistled the play dead. Plante lay on the ice, out cold from the pain, his blood pooling around him. After he was taken off the ice and stitched up by the arena physician, Plante must have secretly smiled to himself because now he had an excuse to use his mask, and Blake could say nothing to stop him. Sure enough, after taking one look at his goaltender's broken and bloody face, Blake conceded defeat:

"Wear your mask if you want, Jacques." Plante had won.

Still, some people were slow to get used to the idea of masked goaltenders. Arturo F. Gonzales, in an article published in *Modern Man Magazine* in 1960, described Plante's appearance:

> *Crouched in the cage with the sun-white glare of hockey rink floodlights carving his artificial "face" into deeply shadowed eye sockets and a gaping hole of a "mouth," Plante looks like something out of a Hollywood horror film. And when he uncoils and catapults from his cage toward an opposing player…his image stirs butterflies in the stomach of his target.*

According to long-time Montréal Canadiens broadcaster Dick Irvin Jr., "Plante was the happiest guy in the rink that he got cut [in the nose]. Don't ever feel sorry for him because he was looking for the opportunity."

## THE MASKED JAPANESE GOALIE

Often forgotten between Benedict and Plante because he was not in the NHL, or even from North America, for that matter, is the little-known Japanese goaltender named Teiji Honma who was one of the first goalies to don mask-like protection. A member of the 1936 Winter Olympic hockey team, Honma was 25 years old when he travelled to Garmisch-Partenkirchen, Germany, to represent his country in the hockey tournament.

Not wanting to get a puck in the face because he wore glasses, Honma adapted the style of mask worn by baseball catchers. Made from leather, the mask also had a wire cage to protect the face, and Honma wore it during both of Japan's games.

Just like anything that involves change, complete acceptance takes time, and goalies were slow to adopt the mask, even after Plante's lobbying. But as time passed and the stigma attached to wearing a mask faded, goalie helmets became standard equipment. At first, most masks were simple, white, fibreglass shells with holes cut out for the eyes, nose and mouth (à la Jason from *Friday the 13th*). One of the first players to put a design on his mask was Boston Bruins goaltender Gerry Cheevers. Not satisfied with the plain white mask, Cheevers painted stitches on his mask every time he was hit in the face to indicate where the puck had left a scar. Afterward, goaltenders across the league started to paint all sorts of designs on their masks,

**QUICK FACT:** The last NHL goaltender to play without a mask was the Pittsburgh Penguins' Andy Brown. He last wore the mask on April 7, 1974, in a 6–3 loss to the Atlanta Flames.

to the point where it's now standard practice in the NHL.

The helmet itself continued to be moulded from fibreglass throughout the 1970s. In the 1980s, some goaltenders preferred to use a regular player's helmet with a metal cage attached to the front for protection, but this idea gradually gave way to the hybrid mask goalies wear today. Now, moulded composite materials are used to protect the majority of the face while a metal cage shields the eyes.

## The Hockey Net

When hockey was first played on the frozen ponds and rivers of eastern Canada, to get a goal, a player shot the puck through two rocks, or something else heavy enough to remain in place on the ice. This method was good enough for an outdoor pickup hockey game, but when the sport was organized into leagues, the rocks were replaced by two metal posts of about 1.21 metres in height that were planted firmly into the ice surface.

When hockey moved indoors and competition increased, it was clear these simple metal posts were no longer going to work. The first issue was that is wasn't always easy to tell when a goal was scored. A player could shoot the puck at the "net" and miss completely, but a goal might be called if the puck appeared to the goal judge to have gone in. Also, there were no boards around indoor ice surfaces, so the puck flew all over the place after it went through the goalposts. For obvious reasons, spectators weren't overly eager to stand near the goalposts, so, in order to divert lifted and long shots from going places they shouldn't, the posts were often turned 90° away from the action on the ice. This was, however a method most often used before the arrival of leagues like the Amateur Hockey Association of Canada (established in 1886) and the Canadian Amateur Hockey League (founded in 1896).

It seems obvious that netting was the easy solution to everyone's problems, but it took decades for the first net to appear in league play—even after lacrosse and ice polo had been using netting for some time.

In December 1898, tired of having unreliable goal judges standing at the sides of the goalposts, the Québec Hockey Club of the Canadian Amateur Hockey League (CAHL) proposed a design that placed hanging netting behind the 1.21-metre-high posts that served as the goal markers. The CAHL members liked the idea but worried that the netting would interfere with play behind the goalposts. The netting was proven successful in game play, however, and was adopted for the

1899 CAHL hockey season. It didn't take long for the invention to spread to other leagues.

The crossbar was eventually introduced in the early 1900s, and after that the hockey net didn't change for several decades until Fred Marsh came along and ushered in the Marsh Peg in the 1980s.

As the speed of the hockey game increased during its development in the 20th century, many players injured themselves skating uncontrollably into the goalposts, which were, as mentioned, firmly planted in the ice. Players and coaches knew this was a problem, but no one was coming up with any ideas, either—hockey nets simply needed to be rooted in the ice or else they would move and lift at the wrong time in games. Fred Marsh, however, came up with the solution.

Marsh had always dreamed of being in the NHL, but like so many others before him, he just didn't have the talent to make it to the big leagues. He stayed closely involved with hockey, however, spending over 40 years in rinks around BC, driving Zambonis, taking care of ice surfaces and managing arenas. During this time, Marsh saw his fair share of injuries because of anchored nets. Nets had even shortened the careers of a few top NHLers—both Bill Clement and Serge Savard had crashed into the posts one too many times, suffering knee injuries they eventually couldn't bounce back from. Deciding enough was enough, in the late 1980s, Marsh invented the Marsh Flexible Goal Peg. Instead of the inert metal rods of the goalposts, Marsh Pegs allowed the net to move when bumped during play. When a player crashed into the net, it popped off the pegs and could be replaced within seconds. Marsh Pegs are now the standard in the NHL, throughout most arenas in North America and in many parts of Europe.

## The Father of Referees

When hockey was formalized into a game with set rules, it's no surprise the need for a referee was one of the next changes the sport faced. Fred Waghorne was one such pioneer.

Born in England in 1866, Waghorne moved to Canada as a young man, and while he became involved in sports, it was hockey that piqued his interest the most. Waghorne began playing the sport in the Toronto Lacrosse Hockey League (TLHL), a four-team organization that played lacrosse in the summer and hockey in the winter. The TLHL eventually became the Toronto Hockey League, as hockey took over lacrosse in popularity. The league eventually disbanded completely, but Waghorne continued to be part of the city's hockey culture. In his late 20s and unable to keep up with the younger men on the ice,

Waghorne became a referee in Toronto, and he continued in the job right up until his death in 1956 at the age of 90. Before Waghorne, a designated referee to watch over league games did not exist. It was often a job given to another player, and the position wasn't treated with much respect. Waghorne changed this mentality by making refereeing his job. But being a referee in Waghorne's time was not an easy task because the ref had to perform many duties on the ice. There were no linesmen to break up fights or "face" the puck, and the lack of certain technologies made the job all the more challenging. In the book *Kings of the Ice: A History of World Hockey* by Andrew Podnieks, Pavel Barta and Dmitri Ryzkov, Waghorne said:

> *A few of the rinks were lighted by coal oil lamps, and the corners were dark pockets. It was in rinks of that type that the art of puck-lifting was at its peak. The Pete Charltons* [tricksters] *of the day lifted the puck up to the rafters, beyond the goalkeeper's vision. Often the rubber seemed to drop from the roof, right in front of the surprised goalkeeper, then bounced crazily into the net. Some of the players could lift the puck from end-to-end.*

There was no such thing as glass partitions or arena security, either, and the referees were usually the target of irate fans' wrath, meaning they often had to fight their way out of arenas after games were over. Neither was refereeing a well-paying job, and Waghorne often found himself in remote areas of Canada, having to wait days before moving on to the next city. But he hung on, changing the game in the process.

In the 1800s, to signal the stoppage of play or a penalty, the first referees used a cowbell, but a lot of the spectators at games worked on farms and they often brought cowbells of their own, making it difficult for players to know when the real bell was being rung. Because of this problem, Waghorne introduced the whistle.

Waghorne's innovative ways didn't stop here. During a game in Arnprior, Ontario, in 1900, he made another contribution to hockey that also changed the game forever. At the time, common practice dictated that when a referee wanted to have a faceoff, he placed the puck between the two centremen and play started immediately, usually with the ref's shins and ankles getting hacked to pieces in the process. Waghorne was tired of the bruises, so he decided during the game in Arnprior to drop the puck about a metre above the ice, allowing him a precious second to jump out of the way. The players liked the new move—and so did referees all over Canada. Soon, Waghorne's faceoff puck-drop was a bona fide part of the game.

Waghorne refereed over 2400 hockey games in his career, and in honour of his contributions to the game, he was elected into the Hockey Hall of Fame in 1961 in the builder category. Thanks to Waghorne, the institution of the hockey official became part of the game's legitimization, which helped spread hockey's popularity across Canada. Without the on-ice official, hockey would have remained a game played for fun. Sure, the referee's job, at first, was watching for goals and dropping the puck for a faceoff, but as professional teams arose, leagues needed a core of referees to ensure the game was played according to the rules. Hockey has grown in the NHL from one on-ice official to four, with a whole department of off-ice officials who monitor the game via television. But, essentially, the base job description of the referee has not changed much since the early days—ensure the players respect and follow the rules of the game.

## The Goal Judge

In every NHL arena, there still sits a single man behind the glass, staring at the ice, waiting to push a button to signal if a goal has been scored. This man's job seems almost redundant because of video replay. "Almost" because the NHL just can't seem to find another way to get that red goal light to go off. When hockey was in its infancy, however, the goal judge was one of the most important men in the game.

Originally called goal umpires, these brave souls, dressed in their heavy winter gear, stood a few steps away from the "net," watching for the moment when the wooden puck crossed the goal line. The goal umpire then signalled a goal by ringing a bell. It wasn't always the easiest of jobs. When important games were on the line, goal umpires and judges, like referees, were often the target of volatile fans and angry players. For example, the Montréal Canadiens' Aurèle Joliat, a star player from the 1920s and 1930s, once jumped over the boards and punched the goal judge because he had disallowed a goal in a major game. It took several referees and arena security to pry Joliat off the judge. It was because of incidents like this that goal judges were eventually moved into protective cages, where they remain, more or less, today. Now, however, the pressure on goal judges is practically nonexistent because of the invention of video replay, and they can sit and press their little red buttons in peace.

# Chapter 4

## Lord Stanley of Preston and His Cup

The Stanley Cup, the Holy Grail, the Cup, Lord Stanley's Mug—all names for one of the most recognizable trophies in sport. But the Cup is more than a mere trophy, it's the ultimate symbol of accomplishment for anyone who has ever picked up a hockey stick. There are a couple thousand names engraved on the Stanley Cup, but beyond those names are countless numbers of men who have tried and failed in the pursuit of making it in pro hockey and eventually earning the right to hold the trophy high above their heads.

For those who have been fortunate enough to win the Cup, it's more than just a prize—it's a symbol of all they have put into the sport and all they hoped to achieve.

When Frederick Arthur Stanley, Earl of Derby, Lord Stanley of Preston, was first appointed governor general of Canada by Queen Victoria in 1888, he had never seen, let alone heard of, the sport of hockey. But that year, during the Englishman's first winter on Canadian soil, he was invited to the annual Montréal Winter Carnival. In addition to various activities, Lord Stanley was invited to watch a game of ice hockey between the Montréal Victorias and the Montréal Amateur Athletic Association. The two teams put on an exciting match for the new governor general, with the Victorias triumphing by a final score of 2–1. Afterward, the *Montréal Gazette* reported that Lord Stanley "expressed his great delight with the game of hockey and the expertise of the players."

Back in Ottawa, three of Lord Stanley's sons (Arthur, Edward and Victor) took up the Canadian game seriously, and by 1889 they were all members of the local Ottawa Rideau Hall Rebels hockey team. Naturally, Lord Stanley became a supporter of Ottawa hockey, and even had his own private box at Dey's Skating Rink, home ice of the senior-league Ottawa Generals, whom he regularly enjoyed watching.

After three years of cheering on his sons and the local clubs, Lord Stanley noticed the game lacked something that other sports in his native England had—a trophy, something that

teams from across Canada could compete for
and aspire to attain. Setting his plan in motion,
Lord Stanley sent a letter to the victory celebration held on March 18, 1892, for the champion
Ottawa Hockey Club. He could not attend in
person because he was back in England for the
funeral of his brother, the 15th Earl of Derby.
Stanley was to succeed his brother as the 16th
Earl of Derby, so as a result, his time in Canada
was finished. Therefore, a man who went by the
title of Lord Kilcoursie read aloud Lord Stanley's
letter on behalf of the governor general:

> *I have for some time past been thinking that
> it would be a good thing if there were a chal-
> lenge cup which should be held from year to
> year by the champion hockey team in the
> Dominion.*

> *There does not appear to be any such outward
> and visible sign of championship at present, and
> considering the general interest which the
> matches now elicit, and the importance of having
> the game played fairly and under rules gener-
> ally recognized, I am willing to give a cup
> which shall be held from year to year by the
> winning team.*

> *I am not quite certain that the present regu-
> lations governing the arrangement of matches
> give entire satisfaction, and it would be worth*

*considering whether they could not be arranged so that each team would play once at home and once at the place where their opponents hail from.*

*Governor General of Canada, His Honourable Lord Stanley of Preston*

Lord Stanley commissioned London, England, silversmith G.R. Collis and Company to create a trophy for 10 guineas, about $1250 today. Engraved on the side of the Cup were the words "Dominion Hockey Challenge Cup," and on the opposite side, "From Stanley of Preston." In order to guarantee his

> **QUICK FACT:** The company that originally made the Stanley Cup is still around. They are now called Boodles and Dunthorne Jewellers.

protocol in awarding the Cup was followed, Lord Stanley drew up five preliminary regulations:

1. The winners shall return the Cup in good order when required by the trustees so that it may be handed over to any other team, which may win it.

2. Each winning team, at its own expense, may have the club name and year engraved on a silver ring fitted on the Cup.

3. The Cup shall remain a challenge cup, and should not become the property of

one team, even if won more than once. [Added because, at the time, it was common practice to allow a team to permanently keep a trophy if it won the prize several years in a row.]

4. The trustees shall maintain absolute authority in all situations or disputes over the winner of the Cup.

5. If one of the existing trustees resigns or drops out, the remaining trustee shall nominate a substitute.

Sheriff John Sweetland and newsman Philip D. Ross were appointed the first trustees of the Cup, and thus, Lord Stanley had created one of the most enduring symbols in sport. But he never once witnessed the awarding of his Cup. In fact, Lord Stanley never returned to Canada after he left.

## The First Recipients of the Cup

Creating the Cup was easy. Giving it away for the first time, however, proved difficult.

When the Stanley Cup was first introduced, it was a challenge cup, meaning one team had to have it in its possession in order for another team to challenge for it. The idea itself was all well and good, but carrying it out that first year posed a problem—no previous winner meant there was no one for another team to challenge. The trustees decided to forgo the challenge trophy regulation for the Cup's debut year and instead award the trophy to the winner of the Amateur Hockey Association (AHA) tournament at the end of the 1893 season. It was a tough finale for Lord Stanley's favourite Ottawa Hockey Club, as they lost the championship by one point to the winners, the Montréal Hockey Club. This was the first and only time the Cup was won outside of the playoff format, but all the trustees had to do was simply hand over the Cup to its rightful owners, and everything for that season would be sewn up.

However, when one of the Cup trustees travelled to Montréal to award the trophy, the chairman of the Montréal Hockey Club was out of town, so the Montréal Amateur Athletic Association (MAAA), the association the Hockey Club was affiliated with, accepted the Cup on the Montréal Hockey Club's behalf. Unfortunately, this gesture infuriated the members of the team because they felt the Cup was theirs and should never have been in the possession of the MAAA, so they refused to accept the trophy, asking that it be sent back. The members of the MAAA, all upper-crust Englishmen, weren't about to let a club they were associated with refuse a trophy awarded by the representative of the Queen. They convened in an emergency gathering on how to deal with the crisis and marked down their response in the meeting's minutes: "In order not to offend the former governor general of Canada and not to seem ungrateful in the public's eye, the directors decide to retain possession of the Stanley Cup."

Six months after initially being offered the trophy, the Montréal Hockey Club accepted the Cup, so as not to further embarrass the club.

After these early hiccups, new regulations were installed, and in 1894, the Montréal Hockey Club (now playing harmoniously under the banner of the MAAA) played the Montréal Victorias in the first official playoff game in history. Played on St. Patrick's Day, the first Stanley Cup challenge was won, 3–2, by the Hockey Club. They were then challenged by the Ottawa Capitals later in 1894, and Montréal won again, retaining the Cup title. What followed after this first series was the start of the Challenge Cup era.

## The Challenge Cup Era

From 1893 to 1912, the Cup, in principle, was open to any challengers who thought themselves worthy enough to take it from the champions.

This meant that any team hastily cobbled together could have the chance to get their names engraved on the Cup—for example, a team from an amateur league in Manitoba could challenge the previous Cup champions from Montréal. Lord Stanley never meant this to be the case, even though something similar to the Manitoba versus Montréal scenario occurred on more than one occasion.

## The Dawson City Expedition

In 1905, the Stanley Cup was barely 12 years old, but it was already the defining symbol of Canadian hockey. In this spirit, a group of ragtag adventurers from Dawson City, Yukon, made history that same year by challenging the famed and fierce Ottawa Silver Seven for the right to be named Cup champions.

The late 19th and early 20th centuries saw Dawson City filled with an eccentric bunch of characters who had made their way north in search of fortune during the infamous gold rush. Stories of men plucking big chunks of gold from icy rivers and stumbling across vast reserves of gold deposits just a few metres under the soil were the stuff of legends. Tales of striking it rich in the Yukon spread across North

America and attracted all sorts of enterprising men and women.

One such larger-than-life character was Joseph Whiteside Boyle, a man whose passion for money and sports were synonymous. Having made a decent amount of money in the animal feed business in the late 19th century, Boyle decided to switch careers and manage a boxing club in Toronto, where he sat ringside for Australian boxer Frank "Paddy" Slavin. The two toured North America, setting up fights in different cities, but the life of a travelling boxer was proving hard on the wallet, so after visiting Juneau, Alaska, and hearing whispers of gold in the mountains and hills of the Yukon, Boyle and Slavin decided to set up camp.

The pair quickly secured a 13.3-kilometre section of land along the Klondike River and set to work panning the frigid waters for their fortune. It wasn't long before Boyle realized that four hands in the Klondike River were not going to pull out the riches he sought. Boyle lobbied the government in Ottawa to industrialize his operations, and by 1904, he was running the Canadian Klondike Mining Company. With his reputation established in the business world, Boyle turned back to his first love, sports.

During the peak of the gold rush in 1897, Dawson City was a town of some 50,000 money-hungry souls with personalities as big as their desires for an easy fortune. By 1900, however, the gold rush had all but ended, and Dawson City's population levelled out, leaving behind a much quieter city. This calmer, more civilized pace was evidenced by the sudden growth of four hockey teams that formed a civic hockey league in the area. One team was made up of members of the Royal Canadian Mounted Police, another was local civil service employees, the third was known as the Dawson Amateur Athletic Association and the fourth was simply called the Eagles. The local Dawson residents took little interest at first, hardly eager to stand out on the frozen shores of the windswept Yukon River, but people came around and eventually believed their local teams were top-quality hockey clubs, with the civil service team standing out as the best of the bunch.

Sheriff Jack Eilbeck, president of the Civil Service Athletic Club, believed in the abilities of his team so much that in 1903 he issued a challenge to the Ottawa Hockey club, a.k.a. the Ottawa Silver Seven, the national defending Cup champions. Despite the fact that the Silver Seven were known as one of the best teams to ever play the game and had one of the greatest players in hockey history, "One-Eyed" Frank McGee, Eilbeck's confidence was not without merit. Civil Service team member Lionel Bennett was a top player when he belonged to a Nova Scotia senior hockey league, and teammate Randy McLennan had played for the Stanley Cup in March 1899 as a member of the Queen's University team.

After taking their time mulling over the Dawson City challenge, the Cup trustees and the Ottawa Silver Seven finally accepted Eilbeck's proposal in September 1904. There was just one issue: by time word of the acceptance had arrived in Dawson City, Eilbeck was no longer president of the Civil Service Athletic Club. He was fired for offering civil service jobs to applicants who could swing a bat better than they could process paperwork—it was Eilbeck's attempt at improving the local baseball championships.

But, with a chance for Dawson City to challenge a team like the Ottawa Silver Seven and potentially gain the attention of the entire country, good ol' Joe Boyle saw an opportunity to have some fun and, of course, make a few dollars. Boyle took over Eilbeck's position and immediately began preparations for the Cup game.

With just one look at the Civil Service team, Boyle knew his men weren't going to stand a chance against the professional skills of the Ottawa players. So, in November 1904, he began putting together a Dawson City all-star team. After a quick selection process that put the candidates through a series of drills and workouts, Boyle selected seven players to be part of his new team. In addition to McLennan and Bennett, he added Norman Watt, Weldy Young, George "Old Sureshot" Kennedy, Hector Smith and, in goal, 18-year-old Albert Forrest, who had never played the position before but was quick on his skates and had young reflexes that were sure to come in handy.

The team was ready, but just a few days before they planned to set out on their long journey to Ottawa, they received two pieces of bad news. The two best players on the team, Young and Bennett, had to withdraw. Young was forced out because of a job conflict, and Bennett didn't want to leave his wife for such a long period because she had not yet fully recovered from being dragged down the street by a buggy the previous winter. To replace Young and Bennett, Boyle settled on reserve players Lorne Hannay and Archie Martin. With his final roster set, Boyle decided the team needed a new name, something that reflected its roots. He rebranded the team as the Dawson City Nuggets.

Travelling in the early 1900s was not easy. The itinerary from the Yukon to Ontario had to be carefully planned out and timed so the team would make it to Ottawa in time for its Cup series. The Nuggets were to travel by dogsled to Whitehorse, then catch a train to Skagway Alaska, then board a boat to Vancouver and make the cross-country journey to Ottawa via train. When all was said and done, the trip was estimated to take two to three weeks.

On December 18, 1904, the players waved goodbye to a cheering crowd that had gathered at the edge of town to see them off. The players left filled with excitement and cheer at the possibility of making history, but just a few hours into their journey, things started to go wrong. Arriving at the trail to Whitehorse, they discovered no snow on the ground, rendering their dogsled completely useless. The players tightened their bootstraps and began the long walk to their destination. The *Ottawa Journal* pityingly reported on the struggle of the Dawson team:

> *The first day the Klondikers covered 46 miles, the second 41. The third day saw some of them struggling to cover 36 miles, some suffering with blistered feet. It may give an idea of the hardship they faced when it is recorded that the temperature went down to 20 degrees below zero.*

Incredibly, the hearty northern men made it to Whitehorse after 10 days of alternately trudging through snow and mud.

The team's bad luck continued when it arrived in town to find that an avalanche had virtually shut off Whitehorse from the outside world. When the snow was finally cleared, the men boarded their train to Skagway, but then found out that because of the avalanche, they had missed their steamship to Vancouver. They had to wait another three days for the next one. When the team was finally on its way to Vancouver, the water began to churn violently, and heavy fog surrounded the boat. The captain ended up overshooting his destination, and the boat ended up in Seattle, causing yet another delay. The Nuggets were eventually able to board their train to Ottawa, and after 11 days on the rails, they finally arrived in Ontario. The team had spent 25 days travelling from Dawson City to Ottawa, just over 6400 kilometres. Weather-beaten, road-weary and on unsteady feet, the Nuggets had just two days to prepare before their series against the Silver Seven was set to begin.

Newspapers across North America had picked up the story of the team's harrowing cross-country journey, and the men had achieved a small level of fame because of it. The Nuggets had survived the distance in one piece, but the most difficult part of their trek was yet to come because the team they were about to face had little sympathy for their opponent's trials and had no intention of handing over the Cup.

The Ottawa Silver Seven were the reigning champions of the Canadian Amateur Hockey League and had held possession of the Cup since 1903. The team had one of the most potent offences in hockey, led by the legendary "One-Eyed" Frank McGee. McGee had lost his right eye during a hockey game and was forced to retire, but he loved the game too much and returned to the Silver Seven, becoming one of game's most famous players.

Despite only being able to see out of one eye, McGee scored 135 goals in his 45-game career with Ottawa. Just five-foot-six, he was blessed with incredible speed and a shot to match, but the Silver Seven's list of weapons did not end with McGee. Alf Smith was known as one of the most bruising players of his time and was the enforcer who created room on the ice for McGee to work his magic. Ottawa also had Harry "Rat" Westwick, a player with blazing speed and daunting ferocity. Case in point: during a game against the Montréal Victorias, he was forced to leave the ice three times because of his injuries, but he refused to quit until a broken bone in his ankle forced him to finally exit the game—and even then he refused to be carried off the ice despite the ankle bone protruding from the side of his skate. McGee, Smith and Westwick all ended up in the Hockey Hall of Fame, so, to say the least, the Dawson City Nuggets had their work cut out for them.

On January 13, 1905, a crowd of 2500 jammed into Dey's Skating Rink on Gladstone Avenue, along with Canada's then governor general, Albert Grey, 4th Earl Grey, to watch the local hometown heroes take on the Nuggets, who were dressed in black sweaters trimmed with gold.

> **QUICK FACT:** Earl Grey tea was not named after Canada's ninth governor general, Albert Grey, 4th Earl Grey. The tea's namesake is Charles Grey, 2nd Earl Grey, Britain's prime minister from 1830 to 1834. Charles was Albert's grandfather.

After the crowd had settled in, the teams lined up at centre ice and prepared for the opening faceoff. The crowd politely cheered as the governor general walked out onto the ice to face the puck.

The game got off to a raucous start as the Nuggets came out fast, attacking through the neutral zone and establishing early command of the Silver Seven end of the ice. George "Old Sureshot"

Kennedy and Hector Smith were the first to get shots off on Silver Seven goaltender Dave Finnie, but the Ottawa goaltender stood strong and kept his team in the game. Ottawa regained puck possession. Frank McGee caught a forward pass and flew by the forwards to take a shot through the defenders. Nuggets goaltender Albert Forrest was up to the task and managed to stop McGee's attempt. Ottawa did not back down, though, and continued to physically punish the Nuggets at every opportunity. After the first 10 minutes of play, McGee had put his team up 1–0.

**QUICK FACT:** The actual game-play of hockey in 1905 was considerably different than what spectators see today. Games lasted for two 30-minute periods, and most players stayed on the ice for the entire duration.

On the very next play, Ottawa's Alf Smith got his stick in Norman Watt's face, leaving an open gash on his lip. Watt dropped his gloves and the two went toe-to-toe, neither coming out looking the better for it. Two fighting majors later, both players were sitting on the bench, waiting out their penalty minutes. The moment his penalty ended, Smith stepped back on the ice and broke in on Forrest to score the second Ottawa goal of the game. The Nuggets knew that if they didn't get up on

Ottawa soon, their chance to get back in the game was going to disappear completely.

The Nuggets' Randy McLennan answered the call for his team when, during a scramble in front of Ottawa's net, he managed to get the puck on the end of his stick and snap a goal into the back of the net. The first half ended with Ottawa up 3–1.

The score was only at a two-goal deficit, but the Nuggets were struggling to keep up with the Silver Seven. The only reason the score wasn't 7–1 at the end of the first period was because of rookie Albert Forrest's all-star performance.

Dawson City hoped to make some early gains in the second half, but Alf Smith took away all hope of salvation by putting three goals past a stunned Nuggets goaltender. The score was 6–1. Beaten down and embarrassed, the Nuggets' frustration showed. Norman Watt got his stick up in Arthur Moore's mouth, cutting him, and then, not finished with the Ottawa player, Watt skated over and deliberately smashed his stick over Moore's head, knocking him out cold for 10 minutes. Unbelievably, the referee decided to give both players 15-minute majors.

While the fighters cooled their heels in the sin bin, Ottawa scored two more goals to bring the game up to 8–1. George "Old Sureshot" Kennedy scored the only other goal for the Nuggets, and the game ended in a humiliating score of 9–2.

The following morning, a *Yukon World Press* reporter filed his story with the headline "Klondike Hockey Team Defeated in Extremely Rough Game in the Presence of Thousands of People." The reporter expanded in his story: "The effect of the long journey of the visitors was shown in their form, for the Ottawas gave evidence of better stamina and superior style."

The fight wasn't out of the Nuggets yet, though, and they vowed to make the Silver Seven pay for what the Dawson City team saw as unfair play by Ottawa. Norman Watt was furious over the rough, dirty style of hockey played by the Silver Seven. He was so vocal in his contempt that he was over-heard openly taunting superstar Frank McGee, proclaiming, "Who the hell's McGee? He don't look like much!" Watt did have reason to question McGee, who didn't factor heavily into the earlier game, scoring just one goal. McGee was known for scoring six or seven goals in one game.

Word spread, and Watt's musings reached the ears of McGee himself. It turned out McGee had good reason to hold back—he was recovering from a broken wrist—but now that Watt had laid down the gauntlet, McGee vowed to let it all out in Game 2.

Not surprisingly, another sellout crowd showed up to watch the drama unfold in the second match. However, if spectators were hoping to see a spirited game, they got a slaughter instead. The Silver Seven played Game 2 to systematic perfection, and McGee was a man possessed. Flying at top speed, he skated and drifted between the Nuggets players as if they were ghosts, scoring goals at an incredible pace. At one point in the match, it was as if he was playing the game by himself, with no goaltender to oppose him. During one eight-minute time period, McGee scored eight straight goals, four of them coming within 140 seconds of each other. The game was a total wash for the Nuggets, and when the final bell sounded, the Silver Seven had handed Dawson City the most monstrous defeat in Cup history. In the two-game series, Ottawa scored 23 goals, 14 of which were put in by McGee. The Nuggets' Hector Smith scored the two lone Dawson City goals. The Ottawa Silver Seven were crowned Cup champions—again.

In an effort to hold on to his team's sense of pride, Joe Boyle sent a message back to the *Dawson Daily News* to try and offer up a few excuses as to why the Nuggets lost:

> *Our team played gamely from first to last, but was dead on its feet. While our men have been*

*traveling, the Ottawas have been put through a course of training, and the players are, of course, in the condition of race horses. The game tonight is regarded by all as a wonderful exhibition of play of a team in perfect condition against a team unfit to play, Tonight's game differed from that of Friday in that it was fast, rough, but perfectly clean throughout. Evidently our boys have inspired the respect of the other players.*

**QUICK FACT:** It is documented that the Silver Seven drank a little too much during their Cup-winning celebration, and on their walk home, one of the Ottawa players threw the trophy in the air and punted it into the Rideau Canal. It was only the next morning when the players woke up that they realized what they had done. Luckily, the canal had frozen over, and the Cup lay in the exact spot in which it had been so unceremoniously dumped.

The Ottawa players might have given the Nuggets respect, but the local papers were a little more realistic in their assessments of the game. The *Ottawa Citizen* said bluntly, "Dawson had the chance of a bun in the hands of a hungry small boy."

However, showing no ill will toward their opponents, the Ottawa Silver Seven hosted a lavish banquet for their guests at the Ottawa Amateur Athletic Association clubhouse and celebrated well into the early hours of the next morning.

## The Heroes Return

In the end, there was no doubt the Nuggets had been thoroughly licked by the Silver Seven, but the story of Dawson City's journey in pursuit of the trophy had captured the nation's attention. Joe Boyle seized onto the publicity and booked the team on an eastern tour through the Maritimes and Québec, and even took them into the U.S. for a series of exhibition games. The Nuggets won about as much as they lost, and after completing their tour, headed back west on the long trip home. On April 5, 1905, several players arrived in Whitehorse (others had left along the journey to return to their families and jobs) and decided to return to Dawson City the same way they left, standing proud on their own two feet. The young

**QUICK FACT:** Joe Boyle was not just a man of sports and prospecting. Years after the Dawson City challenge, Boyle left the Canadian north and headed for the battlefields of Europe during World War I, where he financed his own machine gun company, attempted a rescue of Russia's royal family, the Romanovs, from the Bolsheviks in 1917 and a year later had a love affair with Queen Marie of Romania.

goaltender, Albert Forrest, was the first to arrive in town and was immediately surrounded by the Dawson City townspeople. Their dramatic arrival was the team's swan song, because afterward, the players faded into the pages of the history books. It was also later reported that Boyle made a considerable amount of money from the Cup trip and the team's subsequent exhibition games, but the players never got any money beyond what was originally paid to them.

What the players did receive (apart from a lesson in hockey) was recognition for their participation in one of the most widely known Cup series—a series that was over before it began but still remains part of Canadian hockey history because of how far a group of Canadian men were willing to go to achieve hockey glory.

## Challenge Cups

The Dawson City Nuggets weren't the last underdog, amateur team to aim high against teams with much more skill. In January 1907, the Rat Portage Thistles (later the Kenora Thistles) challenged the Montréal Wanderers and actually managed to win the Cup, despite the odds. Many of the rural teams, such as the Thistles, were owned by wealthy businessmen who wanted to bring the Cup to their towns, and in order to make their dreams a reality, players such as Art Ross, Alf Smith and Harry Westwick were paid to join small teams. The rural squads, however, were only able to retain players like Ross, Smith and Westwick for a brief period before the team returned to obscurity after usually losing their lofty Cup challenges. In fact, only the Rat Portage Thistles managed to wrest the Cup away from an eastern power team. The victory was short-lived, however, because the small club lost the trophy after two months—when the Montréal Wanderers challenged them and won it back in March.

Other challengers that fumbled before the eastern powerhouses included the Port Arthur Bearcats from the Northern Ontario Hockey Association on March 16, 1911; the Berlin Dutchmen from the Ontario Professional Hockey League on March 12, 1910; the New Glasgow Cubs from the Maritime Hockey League on December 27, 1906; and the Brandon Wheat Kings of the Manitoba and Northern Hockey Association on March 9, 1904.

These types of challenges didn't last long in the history of hockey because more and more professional leagues were beginning to appear on the scene. In 1908, it was even decided that the Cup was to be exclusive to pro hockey. But, despite this decision, teams from "amateur" leagues still competed for the Cup. Non-professional organizations like the Alberta Amateur Hockey League had prominent teams and operated like a pro league. Still, the Allan Cup was introduced in 1908 as the trophy for Canada's top amateur club.

By 1914, two professional leagues had appeared as the dominant forces in Canadian hockey: the National Hockey Association (NHA) and the Pacific Coast Hockey Association (PCHA). The two leagues drew up an agreement that their respective champions would face each other for the Cup every year in a Stanley Cup final playoff series. The Cup trustees agreed to sign off on this proposal because of the existence of the Allan Cup and because the Cup needed the prominence of the NHA and PCHA to remain relevant in hockey.

In addition to this major change, a year before the agreement was finalized between the NHA and PCHA, the Portland Rosebuds joined the PCHA. This was significant because it forced the Stanley Cup trustees to change one of their rules so that a team from outside Canada was eligible to win the Cup. But, as time passed, the PCHA started to have financial issues with its clubs and was pushed to merge with the rival Western Hockey League (WHL) in 1924. The new WHL lasted another two years, and in 1926 the Victoria Cougars were the last non-NHL-based team to compete for the Cup. Going forward, no other league played for the Stanley Cup—it was all NHL, all the time, and the Challenge Cup era was over.

# Chapter 5

# Women's Hockey in Canada

When most of us think about Canadian women's hockey, we look with pride to the women's national team and the success they've had in recent years. Canada's women's hockey team has definitely raised the profile of the sport in the new millennium, but women's hockey has actually been a part of Canadian culture since the sport was first played by men in the 1800s. After all, the women weren't going to let the men have all the fun.

When Lord Stanley of Preston saw his first game of hockey shortly after arriving in Canada in 1888, he quickly fell in love with the unique Canadian game. Lord Stanley's wife, eight sons and two daughters also enjoyed hockey, and the family took to the game so much that Lord Stanley had the first recorded backyard rink, built behind his official residence at Rideau Hall. This way, his family could enjoy skating and hockey any time they wanted. Soon, Lord Stanley was hosting games in his backyard because the caretakers flooded the ice daily, providing one of the smoothest ice surfaces in Ottawa.

As mentioned briefly in Chapter 4, three of Lord Stanley's sons played hockey, and they did so on such a regular basis that they formed a team of their own, the Rideau Rebels. The Rebels played in exhibition games around the city and even a few games in Toronto. The Stanley women were also big hockey fans, and one of the lord's daughters, Isobel, is often cited as a player in one of the first all-female hockey games—a game that took place on the Stanleys' backyard rink. Isobel played on a government team versus the Rideau Ladies, and photographic evidence exists to support the claim that this was the first organized women's hockey game; the picture can be found at the National Archives of Canada in Ottawa. It shows several women dressed in long skirts and holding sticks while chasing a puck on the ice. Isobel is dressed in white and appears to be trying to get the puck away from an opposing player. This picture is also quite possibly the earliest photo of a women's hockey game, period, as well as one of hockey's first action shots. There is no date associated with the photo, however, and it's assumed that it was taken sometime in 1889 or 1890.

Shortly afterward, on February 11, 1891, the first report of a women's hockey game appeared in the *Ottawa Citizen*:

> *A ladies hockey match was played at the Rideau rink yesterday between teams as follows. No.1: Miss MacIntosh, Captain; Miss Wise, Munro, Ritchie, Camby, Jones, and White. No.2: Miss H. Wise, Captain; Miss MacIntosh, Ritchie, McClymont, Burrows, and Mrs. Gordon. Number two team won by two goals to none.*

There are other recorded instances of women's games in the late 1890s in eastern Canada, and evidence suggests that Albertan women were likely playing organized hockey as early as 1896.

Admittedly, Isobel and her high-society friends played hockey as a leisurely pursuit, but these first forays onto the ice gave women across the country the idea that they, too, could join in the game that men loved so much. By the early 1900s, women's games were regular features at community arenas and outdoor rinks, and unlike other sports like basketball, women followed the same on-ice rules as men. As the men's leagues changed the rules, so did the women's, but there were still some major differences that weren't dictated by rules but by the culture of the time.

Women in the early 1900s were seen as the genteel, fairer sex, and were supposed to be treated as such. Referees in women's hockey were men, and they coddled the women on the ice as they would at a dinner party. The officials babied the women throughout their games, coaching them and even explaining the rules as if they were children. If a woman—God forbid!—fell, the referee often stopped play and rushed over to offer his hand in assistance. As Wayne Norton details in his book, *Women On Ice: The Early Years of Women's Hockey in Western Canada*, a referee at the Rossland Winter Carnival in BC in 1906 failed to come to the rescue of a fallen female player and was harshly criticized for his ungentlemanly actions.

There were women who tried to break free from their decorous image and instead play serious hockey, but these rebellions were often met with fierce resistance from the male establishment. Brian McFarlane notes in his book, *Proud Past, Bright Future: One Hundred Years of Canadian Women's Hockey*, that when a team called the Love-Me-Littles from Queen's University challenged the male members of the school's team to a pickup game, they were met with a few stern words from the university's archbishop about their "place" in the school.

Women's hockey persevered, but it wasn't a game played in heated public battles for trophies like the Stanley Cup. For the first few decades of women's hockey history, female participation was treated more as an amusement than as serious competition. Here is the crowd's reaction to an early women's hockey game, as reported in the *Ottawa Citizen*:

> *That Alpha and Rideau Ladies Hockey teams can play the game was well demonstrated at the Rideau rink last night when they met in a friendly match. Both teams played grandly and surprised hundreds of the sterner sex who went to the match expecting to see many ludicrous scenes and have many good laughs. Indeed, before they were there very long, their sympathies and admiration had gone out to the teams. The men became wildly enthusiastic.*

This patronization of women's hockey was something females had to deal with far into the 20th century. Women were cautioned away from athletic pursuits that didn't involve household chores. The medical profession even claimed that extreme physical activity, such as that experienced in hockey, could disrupt the menstrual cycle and cause damage to the reproductive system. Becoming involved in hockey had to be on men's terms, and as a result, women's hockey remained on the margins.

The clothing women were expected to wear was particularly restrictive. Early photos of women's hockey show no change in uniform from their everyday winter clothing of long, heavy, ankle-length skirts, thick sweaters and large, tasselled toques—not exactly the keys to speed and dexterity. But men funded the women's teams, so women had to follow the dress code. In *Women on Ice*, Norton points out that not all women minded the rules. BC teams from Rossland and Revelstoke were known to wear the latest fashions or modify their drab uniforms with colourful scarves and accessories.

Men, however, who wanted to see the women play, whether they were in fashion or not, were often barred from being casual spectators. The men most often present were the referee and a pair of goal judges. This minimal exposure to males was to protect the women's modesty in case any of them fell down, and to keep the mockery to a minimum—it was just entertainment, after all. As a result, many early women's games were poorly attended, and any reports that exist often focus on the men's pleasure (if they could get into a game) in seeing the women get a little rough. This brought attention to the women's game, but it was the wrong kind.

It wasn't until the start of World War I that women began to question the dainty requirements of women's hockey and start to make changes. First to be addressed was their clothing. Hemlines went up, and skirts were made out of lighter fabrics. Wartime didn't lend practically to women being their "usual" demure selves, and by the time World War I finished, women's hockey teams had completely switched to light jerseys and bloomers or culottes—if the war had taught women anything, it was the importance of functionality. Helen Gurley, who played on the University of Toronto women's hockey team, explained their new attire in McFarlane's book, *Proud Past, Bright Future*:

> *The bloomers came in at the end of the war. In the early twenties they were shortened to just above the knee. By the late twenties, we started to wear a hockey pant that was similar to the pant they wear today except that they were narrower and not as well padded. In my day some of the girls wore small shin pads or even magazines under their long stockings.*

During the Roaring Twenties, two of the best women's teams in Canada's east were the Ottawa Alerts and the North Toronto Ladies. They had dominated all other Ontario teams in the 1921–22 season, and in March 1922, the two teams met in a home-at-home series to decide the winner of the provincial championship. According to the *Toronto Star*, over 4000 fans witnessed the women play to a scoreless tie in the first game, during which the fans "waxed very enthusiastic over the superb hockey displayed." The Ottawa-Toronto series was hotly contested, and tempers ran high by the time the teams met in Toronto for their final game. However, despite the wide interest in this series, a *Toronto Star* reporter who wrote a lively piece describing the game couldn't quite keep his condescending tone hidden:

> Several players "took the count" from heavy checks and Miss Marion Giles, a little tot on the Ottawa team, received a gash over the eye when Miss Mitchell, a North Toronto defence player, bumped her as she shot on goal. The smallest member of the Ottawa team, Miss Shirley Moulds, a 15-year-old youngster with her hair down her back, was the best player on the ice but she couldn't stand up under the heavy bodying of the Toronto girls.

The North Toronto Ladies took the game by a score of 1–0 and claimed the championship. On that North Toronto team, though, was one of the best female hockey players of her time, and one of the most famous Canadian athletes in the country's sporting history—Fanny "Bobbie" Rosenfeld.

Rosenfeld is most well known for her success during the 1928 Olympic Summer Games in Amsterdam, where she won the silver medal in the 100-metre sprint and the gold medal in the 4×100-metre relay. But long before she was winning medals on the track, she was scoring goals on the ice. Described by newsmen at the time as the "superwoman of ladies hockey," Rosenfeld could skate faster than many men and was known for her incredible stickhandling ability. Her skills on the ice were so far above those of her teammates that she was often left alone to do most of the work. She led her teams through some of the roughest and most entertaining women's hockey of her time, but she cut her hockey career short to focus on training for the Summer Olympics. In 1929, however, when suffering from arthritis and no longer able to train for her sprinting events, she recovered enough to return to her first love, hockey. In the end, her dedication to all things athletic earned her the unique distinction of being named Canada's Woman Athlete of the Half Century in 1950.

Perhaps thanks to Rosenfeld's celebrity in the 1920s, women's hockey leagues blossomed across the country, as well as pulled in a steady crowd at the gates. The women's hockey game in North America became so accepted as a whole that in February 1925, the popular American magazine the *Saturday Evening Post* featured a well-dressed female hockey player on its cover.

Unfortunately, during World War II there was a decline in women's hockey as many females entered the workforce yet again to replace the men who were fighting abroad. At the time, everyone assumed women's hockey was bound to return to the popularity it enjoyed before the war, but, unexpectedly, things regressed. The opposition to women playing such a rough game came back, and this attitude lasted for decades.

Not surprisingly, then, interest in women's hockey dwindled, but that didn't stop women from trying to revive it—namely, Toronto's Abigail Hoffman. In the 1950s, Hoffman was a talented eight-year-old hockey player, but no girls' hockey leagues existed. Undaunted, and with the help of her parents, Hoffman cut her hair and was registered as "Ab Hoffman" on her local boys' team. She played the entire season on defence, and no one caught on to her disguise. She was strides ahead of her teammates and was selected to play on her league's all-star team that travelled around Ontario playing in several high-profile tournaments. The only issue was that in order to get certification to play on the all-star team, she had to submit her birth certificate. Once she did, she was discovered and immediately kicked off the squad. Her family tried to fight the decision in court, but the league's ruling was upheld. By that time, though, she had attracted the interest of the media, and her story ended up in *Time* and *Newsweek*. Hoffman never did go any further in hockey but instead ended up on four Olympic teams as a track and field athlete. In 1976, she carried the Canadian flag at the opening ceremonies of the Montréal Olympic Games.

Despite Hoffman's story, negativity in women's hockey persisted at least until 1970, when Vince Leah, in his book, *A History of Hockey in Manitoba*, published that year, wrote:

> *I suppose there must be a page for women's hockey in this book, although it is generally agreed it is not a game for girls and such teams as basketball, field hockey, volleyball and softball are more in feminine line.*

He does speak of a slight revival of interest in women's hockey because of one female player named Allen Rouse, but he adds a jab at the end of his thought: "But in time the girls went back to their basketball, curling and bowling and left hockey to their men folk."

It wasn't until the 1990s that women's hockey finally achieved a concrete level of respect in the sporting world. The turning point began with the first Women's World Hockey Championship in 1990, scheduled to take place in Ottawa, Ontario. But because women's hockey had long existed in the shadows of the more popular and well-funded men's programs, when it was finally announced that the first official Women's World Hockey Championship was actually going to happen, Canada had to scramble to put together a team. There was nothing available that ranked or evaluated individual female players, there were no training camp records—there was nothing. Coaches had to be hired, players needed to be found and money had to be made if Canada was going to show the world that hockey was its game. Everything came together, however, and the Canadian Women's National Team prepared for the international spotlight.

After donning their unfortunate fluorescent-pink uniforms, the Canadian women's team arrived for their first game of the tournament, but the event was not well attended, and press coverage was given more out of curiosity than anything else. If it weren't for the families and friends of the players, the buzz in the arena would have seemed more like a local PeeWee championship than that of an international event. The Canadian women didn't let the atmosphere get them down, and they ended up dominating their opponents, scoring 61 goals and only allowing 8 in return. That year was also the beginning of the Canadian women's heated hockey rivalry with the U.S., and in the final, Canada defeated its southern neighbours 5–2 to win the gold medal.

The Canadians ruled the international hockey roost throughout most of the 1990s, and players such as Hayley Wickenheiser, Cassie Campbell, Danielle Goyette, Jennifer Botterill, Manon Rheaume and Angela James were a thrill to watch every time they stepped on the ice. In 1992, Québec native Rheaume even played one period with the Tampa Bay Lightning in an NHL exhibition match—the first and only woman to ever do so—against the St. Louis Blues. And, for her efforts, Angela James, medallist in 12 national championships and four world championships, was recently honoured with a 2010 induction into the Hockey Hall of Fame. Wickenheiser, however, is probably the most recognizable star to come out of Canadian women's hockey.

Wickenheiser, a phenom from the age of 16, joined the Canadian national team in 1995 under the distinction of being the "female Gretzky" of her time. She lived up to her moniker, and has been a fixture on the squad as one of Canada's top female scorers of all time. She was also the first woman to play a regular season with a men's hockey team when she joined the Finnish team HC Salamat, playing with them from 2002 to 2004.

During the 1990s, however, the women's hockey program in the U.S. was also steadily improving, and by the time the 1998 Winter Olympics in Nagano rolled around and women's hockey was officially declared a medal sport, the skills of the U.S. were on par with those of Canada. The Canadians ended up losing the gold medal to the Americans in 1998, but they fought back and took the 2002 and 2006 Winter Olympic gold medals in Salt Lake City and Turin, respectively.

The investment in Canadian women's hockey is currently one of the best in female hockey in the world, and many international tournaments often become a one-team competition, with Canada as the star. Canadian women keep getting better, and although their opponents are improving, too, it's not at a comparable pace. The Canadian women's national team walking roughshod over international opponents, with only the U.S. providing a challenge, is the norm. Because of the constant drubbings, the International Olympic Committee said during the Vancouver 2010

Olympics that women's hockey was going to be put on review after the Canadian women waltzed into the final against the Americans and came away with a third-straight gold medal. What this review means is that women's hockey could be removed as a medal sport in the Olympics, but within Canada's national team is a young group of women ready to be the new voice of women's hockey. Players such as goaltender Shannon Szabados and forward Marie-Philip Poulin are ready to take on the fight for their sport, just like so many women before them.

# Chapter 6

# The Minority Leagues

Flipping through the rosters of NHL history reveals few minority-group players who have put on a pro jersey. In a league mostly made up of white players, NHL stars such as Jarome Iginla and Grant Fuhr are among just a handful of minorities who have carved a place for themselves in the upper echelons of professional hockey. But don't let this fool you into thinking a minority interest in hockey has been lacking.

One of the first and most successful minority leagues was the Coloured Hockey League of the Maritimes that was founded in 1894 and lasted until 1930. Consisting of seven teams, including the Africville Sea Sides and the Dartmouth Jubilees, the league was popular not only in the Black community but also among Halifax and area residents. The Coloured Hockey League was an unfortunate necessity, as Black players weren't allowed to play in "white" leagues. And so, in order to survive and constantly bring in new fans, the league had to resort to intermission acrobatics, like jumps and tricks on the ice, to keep the crowd entertained.

The players also had a unique style of hockey that eventually led to a change in the professional league whereby goaltenders were allowed to fall to the ice to make a save. Prior to 1918, professional goaltenders were not allowed to make this play, but in the Coloured Hockey League, it wasn't against the rules for a goaltender to fall to the ice to make a save. The benefits of doing so were obvious, and the change was made. Some historians also claim that a member of the Coloured Hockey League first introduced yet another popular hockey technique; it's possible that Eddie Martin of the Halifax Eurekas invented the infamous slapshot. This is supported in the book *Black Ice: The Lost History of the Coloured Hockey League of the Martimes, 1895–1925*, by George and Darril Fosty. In the book, articles and first-hand accounts are cited of Martin terrorizing the goalies of the Coloured Hockey League with his powerful shot. And, of the league's overall original style of play, the book says, "What we see in Nova Scotia is these isolated communities that grew up around white communities, and they just seemed to develop this unique brand of hockey."

The Coloured Hockey League continued to wow Maritime hockey fans until 1930, when it folded because of a lack of money. Afterward, there weren't a lot of options for Black players to choose from, as far as hockey leagues went. As time passed and the attitudes of society shifted, more and more Black players were allowed into the amateur ranks, but breaking into the NHL as a visible minority was something else altogether.

## The First Asian NHL Player

Born to Chinese immigrant parents in Vernon, BC, in 1923, Larry Kwong grew up playing hockey, just like other Canadians who loved the sport. But, unlike a lot of his teammates, Kwong had to deal with continuous name-calling and rough play on the ice simply because of the way he looked. Regardless, Kwong continued to play hockey, and soon he was one of the best players on the ice. He competed for several years in amateur leagues around BC until he joined the New York Rangers' farm team, the New York Rovers, and led the team in scoring for the 1946–47 season. Then, on March 13, 1948, Kwong got the call from the NHL to play in a game against the Montréal Canadiens. Kwong, however, only got one minute of ice time in his NHL debut, and thus only one minute of time on NHL ice—ever. It was a frustrating moment for Kwong, but that single minute of ice time broke a long history of minority exclusion in the NHL, and it paved the way for future players.

## Sasakamoose Goes to Chicago

Born in 1933 on the Sandy Lake Reserve in Saskatchewan, Fred Sasakamoose did not have much as a child. While the average Canadian kid was hitting the ice with the latest pair of skates and equipment, Sasakamoose grew up using tree branches for a stick and rocks for a puck.

Eventually taken from his home and placed into a government-run school, Sasakamoose had a difficult childhood. Playing hockey was always something he enjoyed, however, and he quickly became the best player in his school. Case in point: by the time he was 14 years old, Sasakamoose had helped lead his school team in winning the 1946 northern Saskatchewan Midget hockey championship.

Sasakamoose's skills on the ice got him noticed, and the Moose Jaw Canucks of the Western Hockey League soon came calling to sign him to their team for the start of the 1950–51 season. It wasn't easy for Sasakamoose, going from the small-town life of the reserve to a "white" city like Moose Jaw. He suffered through many a racist comment but kept his head down and tried to let his game speak for itself. By his second season in Moose Jaw, the taunting had died down considerably because Sasakamoose was by then one of the best players on the ice—so much so that the head coach nominated him as captain of the team. In his second year with the Canucks, not only was Sasakamoose the power centre of the team, he was also the owner of 19 goals and 22 assists in 42 games.

Sasakamoose's skill with the Canucks only reinforced the earlier decision of the Chicago Blackhawks in scouting him for their team. When he was 16 years old, the Blackhawks had him sign a letter for $100, committing him to the franchise when he came of age. At 20 years old, Sasakamoose finally got the call he had been waiting for. Said Sasakamoose of his early NHL experiences on the ice in an interview with Don Marks from his book, *They Call me Chief: Warriors on Ice*:

> *You have a dream. A dream to play in the NHL—couldn't go any higher. The Chicago Blackhawks got a hold of me. They said, "You report to Toronto on Saturday night." Being a Native in this world is very hard. I realized my dream: the NHL.*

Sasakamoose played his first NHL game on February 27, 1954, against the Toronto Maple Leafs, but the bright lights and the fast pace of

Chicago were eventually too much for the man who had grown up in a log cabin. Sasakamoose wanted to be near his family and his young wife, so he played with the Blackhawks for the last 11 games of the 1953–54 season and returned home to Saskatchewan during the off-season. He finished his NHL career with no goals or assists and six minutes in penalties.

## The Arrival of Willie O'Ree

In today's multi-ethnic, multinational NHL, a player's exclusion, because of the colour of his skin, would never happen, but for more than half of the 20th century, that was just the way it was. Herb Carnegie, a Torontonian who played for the Québec Aces of the Québec Senior Hockey League during the 1940s, was widely recognized as one of the best players on his team, but because he was Black, he was denied entry into the NHL. Toronto Maple Leafs owner Conn Smythe once told Carnegie, "Herb, I'd sign you in a minute if I could turn you white." The talent was there, but the will for management to break the colour barrier was not. Then Willie O'Ree came along, the first Black player to push through the glass ceiling of "coloured" hockey.

Growing up in Fredericton, New Brunswick, O'Ree loved to play hockey, and just like most other Canadian boys, dreamed of one day playing in the NHL. But for O'Ree, that dream was a particularly long shot—never before had a Black person played in the NHL. That sad fact did not deter O'Ree from pursuing a career in hockey. As a young man he showed prodigious talent, making it as far as the Québec Aces and playing alongside players such as future NHL star Marcel Bonin. O'Ree's talent was even great enough to get him signed by the Boston Bruins as a prospect. He never expected to be called up, but on January 18, 1958, everything changed. The Bruins asked O'Ree to come up from the minors for two games against the Montréal Canadiens, and even though O'Ree didn't score during his brief time with the Bruins that year, he achieved something that changed hockey forever. Like what Jackie Robinson had done for baseball 11 years earlier, the colour barrier had been broken in NHL hockey. O'Ree remained modest. "I know Robinson had it much tougher," he said at the time.

O'Ree only played 45 games in the NHL, and he spent the rest of his hockey career in the minors, but his accomplishments opened up the game of hockey for a new generation of kids who might never have otherwise considered the NHL a career possibility.

## Important Dates in the History of Minorities in Hockey

**1830s and 1840s:** Blacks begin to participate in an early form of hockey in Nova Scotia.

**1894:** The Coloured Hockey League is established in Nova Scotia.

**March 9, 1899:** The Halifax Eurekas of the Coloured Hockey League of the Maritimes take on the all-white Halifax Chebuctos in the first recorded racially divided hockey game. The Eurekas win the game, 9–7.

**1930:** Because of the Great Depression and lack of support, the Coloured Hockey League ceases operation.

**March 13, 1948:** Larry Kwong is the first non-white player to play in the NHL. He plays a one-minute shift with the New York Rangers against the Montréal Canadiens.

**October 1948:** The New York Rangers invite Herb Carnegie to their training camp for a tryout and offer him a spot in their minor-league system. He refuses the offer that cuts his salary in half from what he makes as a semi-professional in the Québec Senior Hockey League.

**1950–53:** Carnegie plays with the Québec Aces of the Québec Senior Hockey League alongside future legends Jean Beliveau, Marcel Bonin and Jean-Guy Talbot.

**February 27, 1954**: Fred Sasakamoose of the Chicago Blackhawks is the first player of aboriginal descent to play in the NHL after he suits up in a game against the Toronto Maple Leafs.

**January 18, 1958:** Willie O'Ree is the first Black player in the NHL after he is called up by the Boston Bruins.

**January 1, 1961:** Late in the third period of a tie game against the Montréal Canadiens, O'Ree breaks across the Canadiens' line and lets go a low, hard shot that gets past the goalie and wins the Bruins the game. It is the first goal by a Black person in the NHL and is also O'Ree's first goal in the NHL.

**1974:** Mike Marson becomes only the second Black player in NHL history when he suits up for the Washington Capitals. Later that year, when Marson and teammate Bill Riley dress for a game on December 26, it's the first time in the NHL that more than one Black player appears in a game.

**October 1981:** Grant Fuhr becomes the first Black starting goaltender in the NHL.

**May 19, 1984:** Fuhr is the first Black player to have his name engraved on the Stanley Cup when the Edmonton Oilers beat the New York Islanders to take the championship.

**November 2, 2003:** Fuhr becomes the first Black player inducted into the Hockey Hall of Fame.

# Chapter 7

# The Enduring Canadian Franchises—A Short History

Throughout much of the history of hockey, three Canadian franchises have continually been at the forefront of the furor. The Ottawa Senators, Montréal Canadiens and Toronto Maple Leafs boast some of the most loyal fans in all of hockeydom, and that allegiance goes back—way back—to a time when the NHL didn't even exist. The combined histories of these teams are a huge part of what defines hockey in Canada and beyond.

## The Original Dynasty: The Ottawa Senators

Long before the Montréal Canadiens held their first Stanley Cup parade and even longer before the Toronto Maple Leafs were a twinkle in the eye of Conn Smythe, Canada's capital had the Ottawa Senators.

In the late 19th century, hockey was just beginning to be discovered by Canadians, but its popularity grew at an exponential rate. By 1881, students from McGill University had organized what many historians believe to be the first hockey team, and by 1883, several other hockey teams had sprouted up around Montréal, Québec City and Ottawa.

The Ottawa Senators' legacy began after three friends, Halder Kirby, Jack Kerr and Frank Jenkins, witnessed teams from Montréal and Québec City competing at the 1883 Montréal Winter Carnival. The trio decided they could match the speed and skill of the Québec players, and so returned home to Ottawa to form the Ottawa Hockey Club. Unfortunately, the new team had no one to play against, and for the first year of its existence simply held regular practices to prepare for the 1884 Montréal Winter Carnival.

The winter carnival in Montréal was a meeting place for Canada's high society of the time, and the new sport of hockey was the carnival's major attraction in the late 1800s. The elite delighted in the speed and physicality of hockey, and if their team won, it gave them bragging rights over friends and family who supported a different squad. Unfortunately for the Ottawa Hockey Club and its fans, the team's first competitive games did not turn out as planned, as Ottawa lost to the more seasoned Montréal teams. However, the Hockey Club was responsible for a couple inevitable "firsts" in its early years. Nelson Porter, who was mayor of Ottawa from 1915 to 1916, scored the franchise's first goal, and Hockey Club co-founder Frank Jenkins was named the team's first captain. It wasn't until the 1885 Winter Carnival, though, that the Ottawa Hockey Club claimed its first victory, against the Montréal Victorias. Ottawa lost the final, however, to the Montréal Hockey Club.

The Montréal Winter Carnival was a great venue at which to showcase hockey skills, but players from other cities eventually wanted to play competitively more often than once a year, so on December 8, 1886, at a meeting in Montréal between the representatives of several clubs, the Amateur Hockey Association of Canada (AHAC) was formed. The association included the Ottawa Hockey Club, Montréal Victorias, McGill College Club, Montréal Amateur Athletic Association (MAAA) and Montréal Crystals. It was agreed that the season would run from January 1 to March 15 and would operate under a challenge system. This meant that a championship team would face a new challenger each week to compete for the champion title. This system was put into place to accommodate teams like Ottawa because the high cost of travel could not support a regular schedule of games. And so, the challenge system ended up playing out almost like a Stanley Cup final—every week. The first championship team of the AHAC was the Montréal Crystals.

Ottawa played and lost its first and only challenge series during the 1887 season, against the Montréal Victorias. Later that same winter, the Ottawa Hockey Club was forced to shut down operations when its home arena, the Royal Rink, was converted into a roller-skating rink. The Ottawa Hockey Club didn't resume action until 1890, and their revival was thanks to the construction of the Rideau Skating Rink a year earlier.

The Hockey Club faced a problem, though—it was still part of the AHAC, and considerable travel expenses were required to be able to operate in the league. To combat this, Ottawa helped found two new leagues, the Ottawa City Hockey League (OCHL) and the Ontario Hockey Association (OHL). The OCHL and OHL were part of the AHAC, but only played in a few of its games. Between 1890 and 1891, the Ottawa Hockey Club developed into a formidable opponent that won the Ottawa and Ontario championships and finished the AHAC season with a handful of wins.

After dominating the fledgling Ontario leagues, the club finally had tangible success in the AHAC as it held the championship title throughout the majority of the 1892 season. But, in the final game of the year against the Montréal Hockey Club, Ottawa lost. The defeat was seen as unfair by many Ottawa fans, as the Montréal Hockey Club had only won one game all year--the one that Ottawa unfortunately lost. Most important, though, was that Canadian governor general Lord Stanley of Preston thought the AHAC's method of determining the champion was unsuitable, given the Ottawa Hockey Club's obvious superiority over the Montréal team (and club record that year of nine wins, one loss). Lord Stanley thought the system was unbalanced and decided to offer up a solution, which he presented at the annual season-ending dinner honouring the hometown team. The *Ottawa Journal* was present at the dinner and recorded the evening's events as such:

> *The backs of the menu cards which adorned the tables set for the hockey dinner at the Russell last night explained why the dinner was given. They bore the championship record of the Ottawa team for the past winter, a record as honorable in the making as it was splendid in success. Nine championship matches won; a single match lost, by the*

*narrowest possible shave. Fifty-three goals
taken in championship contests against the
best teams in Canada; only nineteen goals
the other way. This was the record of a genuine amateur team playing for pure love of
sport and treating all comers as they wished to
be treated themselves...After the toast of
the Queen, Vice-Chairman Ross proposed the
health of the Governor-General, who had
shown himself a hearty friend of all healthy
athletics, and particularly of hockey.*

It was then that Lord Kilcoursie stood and read aloud the letter Lord Stanley had written outlining his proposal for the need of a new way of determining the best hockey team in Canada. To the winner, a trophy was to be awarded, and this prize, of course, came to be known as the Stanley Cup.

## The Coming of the Silver Seven

The Montréal Hockey Club claimed the Stanley Cup in the trophy's inaugural year in 1893, but it was in 1894 that the first official Stanley Cup series was played. On March 22, 1894, the Ottawa Hockey Club faced off once again against the Montréal Hockey Club in front of 5000 hockey fans crammed into Montréal's Victoria Rink.

The Victoria Rink was not built for hosting such a large crowd, and many fans had to sit or stand on a platform just a few centimetres from the ice. The rink was filled with men hoping to see a raucous, physical match, and much to the surprise of the attending *Montréal Gazette* reporter, even the women got into the action. He wrote, "Every lady almost in the rink wore the favours of their particular club," and he also noted, in a poetic manner, "never did belted knight in joust or tourney fight harder than the hockey men."

Ottawa Hockey Club forward Chauncy Kirby managed to push in the first goal of the game, but Montréal answered back with two goals from Billy Barlow and Archie Hodgson. The game ended with a score of 2–1, and Montréal won the Cup for the second year in a row.

Even though the Ottawa Hockey Club had lost, it established itself as the premier team in

**QUICK FACT:** Playing the cover-point position for Ottawa during the 1894 Stanley Cup game was Weldy Young, who later left the team to seek his fortune in Dawson City during the gold rush. When he failed to strike it rich, he was recruited by the Dawson City Nuggets and became a member of the team that challenged his old club in the famous 1905 Stanley Cup series.

the capital region and began to attract a higher calibre of player. The team already had future Hall of Fame legend Harvey Pulford, and before the turn of the 19th century, added other legends such as Alf Smith, Harry "Rat" Westwick and brothers Bruce and Hod Stuart. But despite having these legendary players on the team, Ottawa failed to win the AHAC league championship between 1894 and 1900, finishing only as high as second, albeit several times. Interestingly, it was during this period that the club received the nickname the "Ottawa Senators" and changed its white jersey to the famous barber-pole pattern, set off by the team's signature horizontal black, red and white bars.

From 1894 to 1900, the Montréal Victorias and Montréal Shamrocks owned the Stanley Cup, but as the popularity of hockey spread across Canada, more teams began to challenge for that little silver cup. Ottawa spent its time shoring up its roster, and by 1902, the team had found the right combination of players to challenge for the top spot in their league and, thus, for the ultimate prize. Joining the ranks with Pulford and Westwick were goaltender Bouse Hutton and the Gilmour brothers, Bill and Dave. But the player who brought the Ottawa club up to where it belonged was "One-Eyed" Frank McGee.

A job as a hockey player was not something McGee's family had envisioned for him. He was from a prominent Canadian family, and his parents figured a career in the government was a sure thing in continuing the legacy of McGee's late uncle, Thomas D'Arcy McGee, one of the Fathers of Confederation. Hockey, after all, was the sport of brutes and was considered a pursuit beneath the family's standing, plus it was dangerous. Frank did, indeed, go on to work for the government after his university days, but his true passion was out on a cold sheet of ice.

McGee's love for hockey won out over a career in government, and he began his tenure in the game with the amateur Aberdeens. It didn't take long for him to distinguish himself as one of the best players in the entire capital region, but during the early part of McGee's hockey career, the concerns of his family proved not to be unfounded. While playing with the Aberdeens in a game in Hawkesbury, Ontario, McGee was hit in the left eye by a "lifted puck" and collapsed to the ice in a pool of blood. He never recovered the use of his left eye, but the injury did not detract from his grit or talent on the ice. The Ottawa Senators came calling before the start of the 1903 season and persuaded McGee to join the team. McGee only played for Ottawa for three seasons, but in that time he created a legend that still echoes to this day. With the talent of "One-Eyed" Frank on their side, the Ottawa Senators became the premier team in Canada and ended the domination of the Montréal clubs over the Stanley Cup.

McGee started his season with the Senators as a relative unknown, but by his second game, he had everyone talking. During the game against the Montréal Victorias, McGee appeared to be playing against the entire team on his own. It seemed that for the majority of the game, the puck was found on the end of his stick, so deftly did he manoeuvre around the opposing team. After scoring one goal, McGee received a round of polite applause from the crowd, but after his second, third, fourth and fifth goals, the crowd erupted in full-out cheers for their new superstar. McGee's exploits on the ice continued, and after playing in just six games, he had scored 14 goals and led his team to a first-place tie with the Montréal Victorias at the end of the season. This meant the Senators and the Victorias were to meet in a two-game total-goal series to decide the winner of the Stanley Cup in March 1903. The previous winners of the Cup, the Montréal Hockey Club, failed to finish the season with enough points, thus putting the Cup back up for grabs.

The first game of the series was a defensive affair that ended in a 1–1 tie, but in the second match, Ottawa turned on the offensive jets, led by none other than McGee. Pulling his team ahead with three goals, the Senators finished off the Victorias by a final score of 8–0. The win earned the Ottawa Hockey Club its first Stanley Cup championship and also brought forth a new nickname for the team.

After the game, as the team members were celebrating the sweet taste of victory with more than their fair share of alcoholic beverages, the club manager showed up with a gift for each player—a shiny silver nugget. As word of this generous gesture hit the news media, the papers dubbed the team the "Silver Seven," and the name stuck.

For the next three years, the Ottawa Silver Seven dominated all their opponents and were the winners of the Stanley Cup at every challenge they faced. They were truly the first hockey dynasty the sport had ever witnessed. The Silver Seven played 13 Stanley Cup challenge games in that time, and they only lost two. They also outscored their opponents by 151 goals to 74, despite the team's ever-changing lineup—but they couldn't keep winning forever. In March 1906, the Silver Seven lost their lustre when the

Montréal Wanderers wrestled the Cup from their hands in a two-game total-goal series that Ottawa lost by a final tally of 12–10.

Afterward, the original members of the Silver Seven went their separate ways and the team couldn't bring back its glory days. It was during this period that the name Silver Seven was dropped, and the team permanently adopted the Ottawa Senators moniker.

The Senators began to have a glimmer of better things to come when a young man named Fred Taylor joined the team in 1907. Long before Bobby Orr, Taylor was the first defenceman to be seen as an offensive threat. With the ability to skate backward faster than most could skate forward, it was his use of speed that earned him the nickname "Cyclone" after an *Ottawa Journal* cartoonist depicted him as a cyclone clearing a path to the net through opposing players; so dominant a force was Taylor that he could control the flow of a game just with the skill of his skating and stickhandling. Wrote an observant newsman prior to the start a game between the Montréal Wanderers and Ottawa during the 1909 regular season:

> *The first question asked by the Wanderers players wasn't surprising: "Is Fred Taylor going to play?" Of the men the Wanderers don't want to see on the ice, it is Taylor. His presence means*

*50 percent extra work for them and depreciates their chances by as much.*

The Wanderers were right to worry—the Senators won the season, gaining back the Stanley Cup from Montréal.

## The NHL Years

Up until the creation of the NHL in 1917, the Ottawa Senators maintained their high level of play and won two more Stanley Cup titles in 1910 and 1911. Their lineups throughout those years included such legends as goaltenders Percy LeSueur and a young Clint Benedict, the offensive talents of Jack Darragh and Harry Broadbent and defensive stalwarts such as Alex Currie and Fred Lake.

When the National Hockey Association was disbanded in 1917 and the NHL was formed, the Ottawa Senators were one of the first teams to sign as charter members, along with the Montréal Canadiens, Montréal Wanderers and Toronto Arenas.

The Senators' first year in the NHL was a rather forgettable one, as they placed in the middle of the pack and failed to make it into the finals. But the team's best years were yet to come, and with a lineup of players that included eight future Hall of Fame members, it was only a matter of time before the Senators began to win.

Frank Nighbor led the way for the Senators during the 1919–20 season with 26 goals in 23 games. The Senators finished the year at the top of NHL standings and met up with the Seattle Metropolitans in the Stanley Cup final. The Metropolitans made the long journey to Ontario to play the first game of the best-of-five series on March 22, 1920, at Ottawa's Dey's Skating Rink.

Since the arena had a natural ice surface, the Stanley Cup finals were at the mercy of the weather, and, unfortunately, that week the Ottawa region was hit with an unseasonably warm spring thaw. With the temperature hovering around the freezing mark, the condition of the ice was of prime concern for both sides. When the teams skated onto the ice for the first faceoff, it was obvious the surface conditions were not ideal. In several areas, large pools of water were forming, and after 10 minutes, the players had created enough chips and ruts to make it a rough go for the rest of the game. The teams persevered and managed to work through the conditions, and the Senators came out on top with a final score of 3–2. The weather, however, continued to be a factor in the remainder of the games, and it slowed the play down considerably. Ottawa won the second game, and Seattle pulled out a 3–1 victory in Game 3, but the warm weather was too much and the teams were forced to move out of Ottawa to play the rest of the series in Toronto's Mutual Street Arena on its artificial ice surface. On better ice, the pace of the game picked up, and so did the scoring. The Metropolitans won Game 4 by a score of 5–2, but Ottawa had the last laugh in Game 5, winning easily by a score of 6–1. The overall win gave the Ottawa Senators their first Stanley Cup as a member of the NHL.

Ottawa repeated as Stanley Cup champion in 1921, 1923 and 1927. After that, many of the players who had kept the Senators at the top of the league went into retirement, and the fortunes of the team went along with them. By the end of the 1930–31 season, the Senators were at the bottom of the league and were struggling to stay afloat. The entire NHL was struggling to stay in business at this point because of the effects of the Depression, but the Senators' on-ice product was not helping to get paying fans into the seats. In order to save the franchise from extinction, the unprecedented move of suspending operations for one season was taken in the hopes the world financial market would turn around and, afterward, the team could once again put together a roster of players who could find a way to win.

After sitting out the 1931–32 season, the Senators returned to action at the start of 1932–33, hoping to turn their fortunes around. But, if anything, things were worse, and the Senators finished the year last in the league. The 1933–34 season was no better, and on March 15, 1934, the Ottawa Senators played their last NHL game of the era against the New York Americans to a 3–2 loss. Frank Finnigan scored the final goal of the original Ottawa Senators franchise, and once the season was over, the rights to the Senators franchise were sold to St. Louis, where the team became known as the Eagles.

## The New Senators

After 50 years, nine Stanley Cups and countless hockey legends who were destined for the Hockey Hall of Fame, the Ottawa Hockey Club/Silver Seven/Senators team had certainly left its mark on professional hockey. Ottawa remained a hockey hub, even after the Senators departed, but fans went without a professional hockey team for more than 50 years until Ottawa businessman and hockey aficionado Bruce Firestone, along with friends Randy Sexton and Cyril Leeder, revived the idea of bringing an NHL team back to Canada's capital.

As Firestone told author Joan Finnigan in her book *Old Scores, New Goals: The Story of the Ottawa Senators*:

> *I had grown up in Ottawa and I knew Ottawa had changed. It had grown much bigger, it was more diverse, and it was much richer. I simply believed that it was the logical choice in Canada for the upcoming NHL expansion franchise.*

He was right. It took a lot of work and financing, but the new-age Ottawa Senators returned to NHL action for the 1992–93 season. The first few years were tough going for the franchise, but loyal hockey fans in the capital stuck by their team, and the Senators slowly began to climb out of the league basement. Young players such as Daniel Alfredsson, Marian Hossa and Jason Spezza marked the beginning of a new era for the franchise. The team even had some success in the regular season between 1996 and 2004 but always seemed to fall apart in the playoffs. It wasn't until 2007 that the Senators finally made it back into the Stanley Cup finals—for the first time since 1927. Unfortunately, they met up with a determined Anaheim Ducks squad and the goaltending of Jean-Sebastien Giguere. The Senators lost the series in five games and have not made it back to the Cup finals since.

## Le Club de Hockey Canadien

> *We don't own the team, really. The public of Montréal, in fact, the entire province of Québec, owns the Canadiens. The club is more than a professional sports organization. It's an institution, a way of life.*

> —Senator Hartland Molson (former Canadiens owner)

Hockey in Québec for a long time was the sport of English elite, with the French on the outside looking in. It was English money that financed teams from the province (the majority of which were from Montréal) during the early days of hockey, starting with the first organized game played at Victoria Rink in March 1875. No question, hockey was popular in the French communities in and around Montréal, but it was a sport for kids to play in the streets and on frozen ponds. While teams such as the Montréal Victorias and the Ottawa Hockey Club challenged each other at the Montréal Winter Carnival in the late 1880s, the city's French population never actually had a team of its own. By the time the first Stanley Cup rolled into the city in 1883, there were the English Montréal Wanderers, the Irish Montréal Shamrocks and the Scottish Montréal Victorias, but still no francophone team

Such a team didn't arrive in the city until the early 1900s, when the Montréal Montagnards and the Montréal Nationals joined the Federal Amateur Hockey League. There were great expectations that both of these teams were sure to do well against their English rivals. But after the first season, the Montagnards and Nationals were more like embarrassments than anything else. The Nationals lost every game in their first season—and then folded. The Montagnards lasted slightly longer, but the result was the same.

Unless the money to finance a top team suddenly popped up out of nowhere, it seemed as if the French were destined to languish (far) behind their English hockey-playing counterparts. But then along came the young, rich J. Ambrose O'Brien.

Not a Frenchman at all, O'Brien was born in the town of Renfrew, Ontario, and like many young Canadian men, had been involved in hockey from an early age. However, despite loving the game, O'Brien faced the reality of many aspiring players: he just wasn't good enough to advance beyond an amateur level. So, instead, O'Brien focused on his business and became a powerful silver magnate in southern Ontario. Hockey always remained a passion, however, and since he didn't play, he purchased two northern Ontario teams in Cobalt and Haileybury, and another in his hometown of Renfrew.

O'Brien's acquisitions in the small mining towns in Ontario caused a hockey craze they hadn't seen before. To feed the frenzy, in the spring of 1909, O'Brien and other local business owners financed a series of pro-hockey exhibition games in the area, featuring the Ottawa Senators and Montréal Wanderers. As Trent Frayne writes in his book, *The Mad Men of Hockey*:

> *When the teams returned home, half the players stayed behind to cash in on the bonanza. The whole area was hockey crazy. Tens of thousands of dollars were bet on each game; often thousands changed hands on a single goal. Miners in the crowds fought in the rinks during games and up and down the streets after them, and during that wild period the best hockey players in the world were performing in this backwoods league formed to take advantage of the silver discovery.*

Despite the fan interest, the Ontario hockey market was small, and O'Brien knew the only way to ever get a crack at the Stanley Cup was to join one of the more powerful leagues to the east. He had actually stolen a lot of talented players from these teams, and he knew he had created a couple rosters that might be able to take home hockey's ultimate prize. In fact, earlier in 1909, O'Brien had gotten wind of some unrest within the Eastern Canadian Hockey Association (ECHA), and so he saw the perfect opportunity to set up his teams in a more respected league, as well as get his shot at the Cup.

The problem in the ECHA had developed when the Montréal Wanderers declared they wanted the right to play their home games in their own building, the Jubilee Rink, on the east side of the city. All the other teams in the league wanted to play in the larger, more profitable Westmount Arena, but Wanderers owner P.J. Doran, who also owned the Jubilee Rink, refused to cooperate and was summarily kicked out of the ECHA. The remaining members of the association consequently formed the new Canadian Hockey Association (CHA).

With the Wanderers out of the picture and a space now open, O'Brien approached the CHA in the hopes that one of his teams could take over the spot vacated by the Wanderers. O'Brien was laughed out of the room.

At that same meeting was a man named Jimmy Gardner, an executive for the Wanderers who was trying to persuade the CHA to change its ruling and reinstate his team in the upcoming season's schedule. He failed to move the members in his favour, and after storming out of the meeting, sat down beside O'Brien, who had stuck around in the hopes of getting another chance with the board. The two men got to talking, and Gardner came up with the idea that the best way to get revenge against the CHA that had shunned them would be to set up a competing hockey league. The league, however, had no choice but to be small because there were only four teams to play in it (Cobalt, Renfrew, Haileybury and the Wanderers), so O'Brien and Gardner decided to expand their membership with a second Montréal team. Part of the Montréal hockey scene for many years, Gardner recognized the need for the French community to have a successful team of its own, so he suggested that the new Montréal squad be made up of exclusively French Canadian players. Businessmen at heart, O'Brien and Gardner knew that healthy tickets sales, to say the least, were a real possibility should the team succeed. Following their brainstorming session, the men parted ways and agreed to meet at a later date to finalize the formation of their league and the creation of a new franchise.

On December 2, 1909, a meeting was called in Room 129 of Montréal's Windsor Hotel to put in place the final touches on the new National Hockey Association (NHA). The Cobalt Silver Kings, Renfrew Creamery Kings, Haileybury Comets, Montréal Wanderers and a new Montréal team, le Club de Hockey Canadien (the original name of the Montréal Canadiens) now made up the teams of the NHA.

The Habs didn't immediately change the hockey world. They were simply another team in another league at a time when teams and leagues folded faster than the blink of an eye. Little did anyone know that the Canadiens were to become a cultural institution that was going to last for over 100 years.

**QUICK FACT:** It's a common belief that the letter "H" in the Montréal Canadiens' logo stands for "Habs" or "Habitants," but it actually refers to "hockey," as in "Club de Hockey Canadien." The term "Habs" or "Habitants" means farmer or rural resident, a now-homage to the fact that most French Canadians on the early teams were from the countryside.

## Les Canadiens sont la ("The Canadiens are here")

Jack Laviolette, who had many connections in the French hockey world, was given the task of assembling the Canadiens' first roster for the team's debut game against the Cobalt Silver Kings on January 5, 1910, at the Canadiens' home arena, the Jubilee Rink. In just under one month, Laviolette had managed to assemble quite a competitive team. It had two star players in Didier Pitre and Newsy Lalonde, along with Joe Cattarinich, Ed Decary, Arthur Bernier, Georges Poulin, Ed Chapleau, Ed Millaire, Noss Chartrand and Richard Duckett. The team was in place, and the Canadiens were ready to hit the ice.

Just over 3000 spectators pushed their way into the Jubilee Rink to witness the first NHA game, and, of course, the only all-French pro hockey team to ever exist. Through a heavy layer of cigarette smoke and the raucous applause of the fans, the Canadiens made their debut wearing white pants, red socks and blue jerseys that had a white stripe running from the shoulder to the chest and a large white "C" on the front.

Only 17 minutes into the game, Lalonde scored the first goal in Montréal Canadiens and NHA history. Poulin soon potted another goal, and Montréal was ahead 2–0 before the end of the period. At this point, the game was half over, because in 1910, there were only two periods of 30 minutes each, with a 10-minute intermission. And so, in the second period, even though the Cobalt Silver Kings came back, each time they did, the Canadiens managed to return the favour.

By the end of the game, the score was tied 6–6. Overtime. It only took about five minutes for Poulin to score the winning goal.

The next day, the *Montréal Gazette* wrote:

> *The winning of the match was the signal for a demonstration that recalled old Stanley Cup struggles. The rink was filled with a gathering that gave the Canadiens as loyal support as any hockey team ever received in Montréal.*

The Montréal Canadiens were an instant success, as people spread the word of this new fast-paced, skilful hockey team that just happened to be French as well. It didn't matter that the Canadiens only won two games in their first season—the team's place in the hearts and minds of Montréalers was without a doubt solidified.

O'Brien's and Gardner's larger gamble on creating their own league paid off later in 1910 when the board that had originally refused them entry into the CHA had to fold its league operations and many of the CHA teams simply moved over to the NHA. The 1910–11 NHA season saw the arrival of the Ottawa Senators and Québec Bulldogs just as the Cobalt Silver Kings, Haileybury Comets and Montréal Shamrocks shut down their teams.

That season, the Canadiens added a few players to their lineup, and they had an immediate impact on the team's success. Goaltender Georges Vezina and forward Newsy Lalonde were great assets to the team, but the Canadiens still couldn't quite make the push—they finished their second season behind the Ottawa Senators, missing their chance to play for the Stanley Cup.

In 1911, the owners of the Montréal Canadiens ran into some legal trouble from George Kennedy, who owned a French Canadian hockey team called Le Club Athlétique Canadien that operated in Montréal's east end. Kennedy wanted to get his hands on an NHA franchise, so he threatened to go to court to stop the league from using the name "Canadiens" since he had been operating his team before the NHA existed and therefore laid claim to the title. The Canadiens owners didn't want to go to court and suffer the inevitable bad press, so Kennedy got his way and was handed the team to operate as the Canadiens while O'Brien concentrated his efforts on his other teams. Fortunately for upper management, this change in ownership did nothing to stop the excitement the Canadiens brought to Montréal.

Over the next few seasons, the Canadiens continued to play quality hockey, but the Ottawa Senators were the dominant club and kept the Canadiens from challenging for the Cup, time and time again. It wasn't until the 1915–16 season that things began to turn around. The Canadiens finished in first place in the league, and Newsy Lalonde (who had returned from a stint with the Vancouver Millionaires in 1912) won the scoring title with 31 goals in 24 games. The Canadiens finally had their chance to win the Stanley Cup, and they faced off that winter against the Pacific Coast Hockey Association (PCHA) champion Portland Rosebuds. This playoff series was also the first time a challenger from the U.S. was allowed to play for the Stanley Cup.

**QUICK FACT:** When George Kennedy took over control of the Canadiens, he changed their jerseys from blue and white to a solid red with a large green maple leaf in the centre that surrounded an ornate "C." The look was short-lived; the jersey was changed again after one season.

**QUICK FACT:** To decide the winner of the Stanley Cup, it was agreed that the winners of both the PCHA and NHA would play in one best-of-five series. This format was used until 1926 when the Stanley Cup became the property of the NHL.

## The Habs' First Cup

The Portland Rosebuds had won their league championship over a month prior to the Canadiens winning theirs, and so they arrived in Montréal well rested and ready for the best-of-five series. As per the rules for this playoff, Games 1, 3 and 5 were played under NHA rules, and Games 2 and 4 under PCHA rules. The main difference between the two leagues was that the PCHA played with seven men, one of them a rover, and the NHA with six.

> **QUICK FACT:** The rover was a position that existed during the early 20th century. This player lined up between the three forwards and two defencemen, and, as needed, became an extra attacker or defender.

Since this was the first American challenger for the Stanley Cup, NHA brass hoped the series was going to be a big moneymaker, but what wasn't considered was that the games were being played in Westmount Arena, not the Canadiens' home ice at Jubilee Rink. The change of venue made a big difference in the number of fans who first came out to watch the series. For one thing, Jubilee Rink was located on the east side of the city where the Canadiens' biggest fans—the francophone population—lived. By moving to Westmount Arena, where the majority of

Montréal's English community resided, the organizers quite effectively cut off many of the team's fans. Secondly, the tickets at Westmount Arena were more expensive than what fans were used to, thereby making it difficult for a lot of them to afford the games. For Game 1, only a handful of fans showed up.

The initial lack of fan support wasn't helped by the fact that goal scoring star Newsy Lalonde was battling the flu, and Jack Laviolette was nursing a broken nose. Not surprisingly, the Rosebuds took the first game by a score of 2–0. Portland's score would have been much higher, however, had it not been for the goaltending of Georges Vezina, in what was later described by a *Montréal Gazette* reporter as an "amazing acrobatic performance." For Game 2, both Laviolette and Lalonde decided to sit out, but even so, the Canadiens managed to even up the series with a 2–1 win, setting the stage for a memorable Game 3.

Lalonde and Laviolette returned to the ice, and better rested, they made an immediate impact on the game. By the halfway mark, the Canadiens were clearly dominating the play, and in the hopes of getting his team back on track, the Rosebuds' Ernie "Moose" Johnson took a run at Lalonde. Both benches emptied out onto the ice, and when it was painfully clear that the referees had no hope of controlling the barrage of fists and flailing limbs, the police were called in to stem the violence and return the game to civility. When the broken sticks and blood were cleared away, Lalonde and Johnson were tossed out of the game. Losing their best player didn't end up mattering for the Canadiens—they went on to win the game 6–3.

Word of the violent matchup spread throughout Montréal, and the previously empty Westmount Arena was packed to capacity for the remainder of the series. Portland managed to pull out a 6–5 win in Game 4, forcing a Game 5. It was tense, with the Rosebuds taking the early lead and Canadien Skene Ronan tying the game soon afterward. The rest of the match was a defensive contest between the two teams, but it was an innocent-looking shot from the Canadiens' Goldie Prodgers that beat the Portland goaltender with only a few minutes remaining on the clock, making the score 2–1. When the final second ticked away, the Montréal Canadiens had won their first Stanley Cup. For their efforts, George Kennedy gave his players a $238 bonus.

## Into the NHL

When the NHA was disbanded in 1916 and the NHL was formed a year later, only four teams—the Ottawa Senators, Montréal Canadiens,

Toronto Arenas and Montréal Wanderers—made the transition into this new era of hockey. The NHL, starting out on shaky financial ground because of its lack of teams, was put in even more jeopardy when the Westmount Arena, home of the Wanderers, burned to the ground. The Wanderers, already in the red, lost all their equipment and couldn't afford to continue operations. The team officially withdrew from league play after just six games in the 1917–18 season.

The Québec Bulldogs were also supposed to transition from the NHA to the NHL, but ended up disbanding, too, because of World War I and because other teams offered their existing players better wages. In particular, the Montréal Canadiens pounced on star Québec forward "Phantom" Joe Malone who had finished the last NHA season with an incredible 41 goals in 19 games with the Bulldogs.

In his first season with the Canadiens, Malone did not disappoint. He was teamed up with Newsy Lalonde and Didier Pitre to form the most effective line in the Habs' short history. In just 20 games, Malone scored a record 44 goals, Pitre scored 17 more in the same amount of time and Lalonde potted another 23 goals in only 14 games. But despite having some of the top scorers in the league, the Canadiens lost the NHL final to the Toronto Arenas, who went on to defeat the PCHA's Vancouver Millionaires to win the Stanley Cup.

The Canadiens returned for the 1918–19 season, determined to again make their mark in the NHL. They swept the regular season and NHL finals, and even though they made it to the 1919 Stanley Cup playoff, it wasn't a team that ended up defeating the Canadiens.

## Influenza Cancels the Cup

The end of World War I was, of course, a time of celebration, but just because the fighting was over didn't mean all the world's problems were solved. In particular, once the soldiers began returning home, they brought with them the illnesses they had picked up in the close, unsanitary confinement of the trenches. A worldwide outbreak of Spanish influenza began in March 1918, and by 1919, Canada—and the NHL—were caught in the thick of it.

The flu was affecting the players, but it also had a large impact on the number of people who came out to watch hockey games. Attendance numbers dropped drastically because of a collective, heightened fear of contracting the sickness—a feeling of panic partly fostered by government warnings to avoid public gatherings. Somehow, though, the NHL managed to push through the season and organize a Stanley Cup final.

## The Pandemic

The Canadiens, while excited about their success during the 1918–19 season, had larger things to think about, thanks to the flu pandemic. At the time, remaining in close quarters for long periods wasn't recommended because of the risk of infection, but the team had to travel to Seattle if they wanted to play out the Cup final against the Metropolitans. In the end, the arguably questionable decision was made to go to the West Coast and thus be confined on a train for several days. Before the team's departure, however, owner George Kennedy insured each player for $1000. When the team arrived, things looked good--all had made it to Seattle without any sickness at all.

Indeed, the good luck continued, and the Metropolitans and Canadiens, evenly matched on the ice, reached Game 4 of the best-of-seven series before things started to turn for the worse. During this game, several of players on the Canadiens team looked tired and pale, and it wasn't the rigours of a hard-fought series that had them looking ragged—it was the first symptoms of the dreaded Spanish flu.

In Game 5, the Canadiens laboured their way to a 4–3 overtime victory to tie the series. (Game 4 had ended in a tie, and at the time, the NHL only played one overtime period in the playoffs, and since neither team scored a goal in OT, no one received credit for Game 4, which resulted in the need for extra games.) Things in Game 6 were not looking good, either—players on both teams had fallen ill, and Canadiens defenceman Joe Hall left halfway through to be taken to the hospital. In the end, six Canadiens players—Hall, Newsy Lalonde, Bert Corbeau, Louis Berlinquette, Billy Coutu and Jack McDonald—and team owner George Kennedy—needed medical attention because of the flu.

It was clear to most that the Stanley Cup final could not go on. When officials announced the series was going to be cancelled, Kennedy asked from his sickbed if he could find replacement players to finish out the games. The Seattle Metropolitans' management refused his request and decided that 1919 would not have a Cup winner—even though Seattle could have claimed the title on the grounds that the Canadiens had to forfeit because of a lack of players. The Stanley Cup trustees agreed with the decision, and after the announcement was made, PCHA founder Frank Patrick sent a telegram to NHL president

Frank Calder informing him of the Canadiens' health:

> *All boys except Hall are doing nicely. Hall developed pneumonia today. He is easily the worst case but we are hoping for the best. Have been here myself for three days and everything possible being done.*

After regaining enough strength, the Canadiens boarded a train back east to recover from their ordeal in Seattle. Hall remained in the hospital because he was still too sick to travel, and just days after the rest of the team departed, the 38-year-old defenceman died.

The unfortunate circumstances surrounding the 1919 flu outbreak didn't end there. Two years later, in 1921, the Canadiens organization was dealt another blow when George Kennedy died in his home on October 19. His death was attributed to complications from the Spanish flu he had contracted during the 1919 Cup finals. His successors, Leo Dandurand, Joe Cattarinch and Louis Letourneau, pulled together $11,000 and purchased the Canadiens from the Kennedy estate.

## The Stratford Streak

Between 1921 and 1923, the Canadiens went into rebuilding mode. They lost several players to retirement and trades, and looked to a new youth movement to bring the franchise back to the top of the league. At the start of the 1923–24 season, the Canadiens acquired a young man from the small Ontario town of Stratford. Howarth William Morenz, a.k.a. Howie Morenz, was a player whose sheer scoring talent elevated the Canadiens to the highest level in the league. Thanks to Morenz, they won the Stanley Cup in 1924, Montréal's second Cup in franchise history and first as a member of the NHL.

With their new, exciting, fast-paced team, the Canadiens began to attract more and more fans to their games, which meant that their home arena would be too small for a successful future. So, in 1924, when it was announced that the Montréal Maroons were joining the NHL, a new arena was constructed on the corner of Ste-Catherine and Atwater streets. It was named the Montréal Forum, and the Canadiens and Maroons shared the space. And, even though the Forum was originally built for the Maroons, it became known as the home of the Montréal Canadiens, thanks to stars like Morenz.

Howie "The Stratford Streak" was one of the most electrifying hockey players of his time and was often called the Babe Ruth of hockey because of his larger-than-life profile on the ice. But the new wave of hope that Morenz brought to the Canadiens could not lift the spirit of the team when in 1925 they lost another member of their family.

At training camp before the start of the 1925–26 season, teammates began to notice goaltender Georges Vezina did not look well. Never one to complain, Vezina dismissed the concerns of his friends and told the team he would be ready to play in the first game of the season on November 28 against the Pittsburgh Pirates. Before the game, the normally cool netminder seemed unsettled before stepping out onto the ice, and as the game got underway, it was apparent something was wrong. Vezina had started with the Canadiens in 1910, and he had yet to miss a game because of sickness or injury, but this time was different. During the first period, Vezina collapsed and had to be carried off the ice. After a series of tests, doctors informed Vezina he had tuberculosis and that his chances of survival were slim. Coming to terms with his fate, Vezina paid one final visit to the Canadiens' dressing room, sat at his locker and wept. He took home the 1924 jersey he had worn when he won the Cup and spent his final days back in his hometown of Chicoutimi. He passed away peacefully on March 26, 1926. The Canadiens weren't the same without him and finished the season in the basement of the league with just 11 wins in 36 games.

Morenz later led the Canadiens back to the top and to two more Stanley Cup wins in 1930 and 1931. The fortunes of the team waned again, however, and the remaining years of the 1930s were a dark time for Canadiens fans. Their team had a few good seasons in the decade, but they were marred by early exits and inconsistent play. Sensing the Canadiens needed new blood on the team, management traded Howie Morenz to the Chicago Blackhawks before the start of the 1934–35 season, and in return gained three players who turned out to be of no lasting value.

After spending one unsuccessful season with the Blackhawks, and then another with the New York Rangers, Morenz was getting too old for hockey and wanted to return to Montréal to end his career with the team he started with. Canadiens general manager Leo Dandurand didn't even pause to think about the decision and traded two minor-league players in order to bring Morenz back into the fold of the Canadiens for the start of the 1936–37 season.

At the first Canadiens' home game of the season, the Forum faithful gave Morenz a deafening round of applause when he hit the ice. Fans loved to see Morenz back in Montréal, but in truth, he had lost a lot of the speed and scoring touch that had made him a superstar. After scoring only 4 goals in 30 games, Morenz contemplated retiring at the end of the season. Fate, however, made the decision for him. On January 28, 1937, in a game against his old team, the Chicago Blackhawks, Morenz chased after the puck into the corner and got his skate stuck between the ice and the boards at the same moment Hawks defenceman Earl Seibert delivered a crushing body check. Morenz twisted and fell to the ice while his leg remained between the ice and the boards. The breaking of his leg was said to have been heard throughout the entire arena.

Afterward, Morenz sat in a hospital bed for two months and fell into a deep depression. Doctors were confident he would walk again, but his career in the NHL was definitely over. On March 8, 1937, however, Morenz's body couldn't keep up the fight, and he died suddenly of what doctors suspected was a pulmonary embolism. Faced with the prospect of never playing hockey again, those who knew Morenz best said he died of a broken heart.

After Morenz's death, the Canadiens spent the remainder of the 1930s floundering at the bottom of the league. The 1939–40 season actually saw their record fall to an abysmal 10 wins, 33 losses

and 5 ties in 48 games—the worst record in the
league. The Canadiens needed another Stratford
Streak to save the franchise.

## The Rocket

Before the start of the 1940–41 season, Tommy
Gorman was brought on as general manager
of the Canadiens, and Dick Irvin was coaxed out of
his Toronto coaching job to take over the bench
of the desperate Montréal team. It wasn't long
after these management changes that things
began to shift back in the Canadiens' favour.
With the addition of a few key players, the Habs
were once again on their way to glory.

First, forward Elmer Lach and solid defencemen
Emile "Butch" Bouchard and Ken Reardon were
signed to the team. Improvement in the standings
turned out to be minimal, and the Canadiens
ended the season only a few points ahead of the
pitiful Brooklyn Americans, but the best was yet
to come with the arrival of a quiet kid from the
Bordeaux area of Montréal.

Maurice Richard lived and breathed hockey,
even before suiting up for the Montréal Canadiens.
As a kid, he would leave his house in the morning
and spend hours down at the local rink, only to
return home when the sun went down. He even
played hockey in his sleep, he once admitted,

always dreaming about scoring that crucial game-winning goal. The scouting reports, however, all said that although Richard burned with the passion for hockey, he was too small to play in the NHL. Coach Dick Irvin disagreed, signing Richard to the Canadiens in 1942. Irvin said he had never met a player so focused and obsessed with scoring. Richard was known to stay after practice for hours just to work on his shot. But to see if Richard had what it took to survive in the NHL, Irvin had resident tough guy Murph Chamberlain put the rookie to the test. With a simple, "Understood, coach!" Chamberlain took a run at Richard during practice and knocked him hard into the boards. Richard fell but rebounded so fast that Chamberlain didn't have a chance to get away before Richard was on top of him, fists flying. It took three players to get Richard off his teammate, but Irvin had his answer. Richard was definitely ready to play for the Montréal Canadiens.

Richard was an instant hit with the tough Montréal Forum crowd. Phil Watson, who played for the Canadiens for the 1943–44 season, described in Irvin's book *The Habs* how the fans welcomed their new star player:

> *One thing I remember is that all those French people in Montréal, they all thought he was*

*the greatest thing from the start. To give you an example, if Elmer Lach scored a goal the guy would announce, "Goal by Elmer Lach." Then Toe Blake would get one and the guy would say, "Goal by Toe Blake." But when it came to Maurice Richard, the guy would start yelling, "Goal scored by MAUUREEEEECE REEEEECHAAAAARD!!!!!"*

Montréal's adoration for Richard only grew, especially during the 1944 playoffs when Richard scored all 5 goals in a 5–1 win over the Toronto Maple Leafs in the second game, of the semifinals. The next day, Montréal newspapers, both English and French, printed the headline, "Richard 5, Toronto 1!" The Canadiens went on to win the Cup that year, defeating the Chicago Blackhawks in four straight games. But it was during the 1944–45 season that Richard accomplished an incredible feat that without a doubt established him as one of the all-time greats of hockey.

Throughout the season, goals seemed to come easily for Richard in every game, and with just a few contests remaining before the start of the playoffs, he had reached the unbelievable total of 44 goals, equalling former Canadien Joe Malone's single-season scoring record. On the night Richard broke the record and scored his 45th goal of the season, Malone was sitting in the crowd at the Montréal

Forum, and he saluted the new star of the Canadiens. Fans everywhere were wondering—could Richard reach the impossible total of 50 goals in a season? It took until the last game of the season, but yes, he could. Richard scored his 50th goal against the Boston Bruins, and instantly, more than a star hockey player, he was a folk hero. As Québec author Roch Carrier later wrote in his famous book *The Hockey Sweater*:

**QUICK FACT:** On the back of Canadian five-dollar bill from 2001, you can find these words, written by author Roch Carrier: *Les hivers de mon enfance etaient des saisons longues, longues. Nous vivions en trois lieux: l'école, l'église et la patinoire; mais la vraie vie était sur la patinoire.* This means, "The winters of my childhood were long, long seasons. We lived in three places—the school, the church and the skating rink—but our real life was on the skating rink."

> *When the referee dropped the puck, we were five Maurice Richards taking it away from five other Maurice Richards. We were 10 players; all of us wearing with the same burning enthusiasm, the uniform of the Montreal Canadiens. On our back, we all wore the famous number 9.*

## The Richard Riot

By the start of the 1954–55 season, the Richard legend had grown to almost religious proportions in the province of Québec. But in the rest of the league, and especially in the eyes of the NHL head office in Toronto, Richard was a spoiled star whose hero status in Québec appeared to give him carte blanche to do whatever he wanted on the ice. Several well-publicized run-ins between Richard and league president Clarence Campbell over what he considered to be Richard's too violent on-ice behaviour were just the tip of the iceberg. Richard's defence for the criticism was that he had always been treated differently within the NHL because he was a Montréal Canadien and, more indicatively, a French Canadian. In a series of articles published in the Montréal newspaper, *La Presse*, Richard openly criticized Campbell for his dislike of the Canadiens and his racist attitude toward the French people of Québec.

Campbell's issues with Richard's penchant for violence weren't completely unfounded. The NHL's list of incidents involving Richard was quite long by the time the 1954–55 season started. In 1951, Richard was fined $500 for harassing a referee in the lobby of a hotel after a game; that same year, he got into an on-ice fight with a Toronto player whom he kicked in the chest with his skate. In that same fight, he punched out another player and was thrown out of the game and fined $50. In 1954, Richard was ordered to pay $1000 for ghostwritten articles in a French newspaper that obviously targeted Campbell as a dictator and a racist. Also in 1954, Richard was fined $250 when he knocked out the two front teeth of the Leafs' Bob Bailey and put his glove in the face of the referee who tried to stop him.

Richard never cared about the fines levied against him because every time they happened, a Québec businessman sent him $1000—a fact to which Campbell later remarked, "Richard could do no wrong in Québec. I was always the villain."

At some point, however, Richard was going to have to be suspended if he kept up his behaviour. General managers and coaches around the NHL were complaining that Richard was getting away with murder on the ice while other players were being fined and suspended for lesser infractions. Doomsday came on March 13, 1955, when Richard was involved in a scuffle that led to one of the most memorable moments in Canadiens and Québec history.

During a game against Boston, Richard got into a fight with Bruins defenceman Hal Laycoe. A violent melee broke out on the ice, and during the rumble, as Richard tried to get at Laycoe, linesman Cliff Thompson tried twice to restrain Richard but was thrown aside. On his third try, Thompson pinned Richard's arm behind his back, and Laycoe was able to get a punch in on Richard. This sent Richard into an even greater fury. He broke loose from Thompson's grip and dropped him to the ice with one solid punch to the jaw.

Two days later, Campbell suspended Richard for the remaining three games of the season, as well as for the playoffs. Montréal newspapers were in an uproar over the harsh suspension. The French papers all had the same hypothesis: if Richard was an English player, he wouldn't have received the same punishment.

The tension was palpable in Montréal as the Canadiens moved closer to the end of the regular season. Their hero had been taken out of the play-offs and something needed to be done. French newspapers across the city voiced their discontent with the suspension almost on a daily basis. Even the mayor of Montréal chimed in on the whole affair. "Too harsh a penalty: Mayor Drapeau hoping for a review of sentence," a *La Presse* headline said, and the *Montréal-Matin* screamed, "Victim of yet another injustice, the worst ever, Maurice Richard will play no more this season!"

Everything came to a head in the final game of the season when the Detroit Red Wings rolled into Montréal on March 17, 1955, and Campbell made the strange decision to attend that evening's game. An angry crowd, gathered outside the Montréal Forum, was carrying signs expressing its hatred of Campbell and the injustice being cast upon Richard. The mood inside the Forum was just as tense. As Campbell tried to quietly make his way to his seat, he was greeted with a loud chorus of boos and the occasional tomato, egg, coin and program thrown at him. Campbell tried to laugh off the attention, but the crowd's focus was so squarely on him that it had hardly noticed the Red Wings were ahead 4–1. At one point, a young man approached Campbell and punched him squarely in the face, and just as security guards were removing the offender from the stands, someone threw a tear-gas canister, sending the crowd into a frenzy. As the angry Forum crowd mixed with the protesters outside, the scene quickly degenerated into a full-scale riot.

Montréal writer Hugh MacLennan, who was at the game that night, later explained the underlying reasons for the riot: "To understand the feelings of the crowd that night is to understand a good bit of the social conditions of Québec of the 1950s." This was more than just a riot over a hockey player, it was about another injustice done to a francophone by the ruling anglophones. There was a strong feeling of solidarity with Richard, and the riots only subsided when Richard himself went on the radio and appealed to the public to return to order.

Despite everything, Richard's suspension remained in place. But even without him in the lineup, the Canadiens still made it into the Stanley Cup finals against the Detroit Red Wings. Montréal lost in Game 7, but as disappointing as the end of the 1954–55 season was, the next few years in Canadiens history were some the greatest of all time.

## Five Cups in a Row

The season following the Richard Riot, the Canadiens returned to action with one of their strongest years to date. They finished 1955–56 with a record of 45 wins, 15 losses and 10 ties—24 points ahead of the second-place Detroit Red Wings. Going into the playoffs was a healthy lineup that included Jean Beliveau, Doug Harvey, Bernie Geoffrion, Dickie Moore, Henri Richard and goaltender Jacques Plante, and the Canadiens easily dispensed of the New York Rangers in five games in the first round of the playoffs. Next up were the Detroit Red Wings in the final, during which the Canadiens got their revenge for their defeat in 1954–55, taking home the franchise's eighth Stanley Cup.

Over the next four seasons, the Canadiens, led by legendary player-turned-head-coach Toe Blake, completely dominated the NHL. In 1960, the Canadiens completed their sweep of the Stanley Cup playoffs without losing a single game on their way to a fifth straight Cup win, a record that will likely never be broken. And, after so many years of giving his heart and soul to the game and people he loved, Maurice Richard decided to retire from hockey that same year.

## The Rivalry Intensifies

By 1960, the Montréal Canadiens had been around long enough and had won enough to earn the team some bitter rivals, such as the Montréal Maroons and the Boston Bruins, but no team's animosity toward the Habs can compare to that of the Toronto Maple Leafs.

The beginning of the rivalry is rather difficult to pinpoint. As long as there has been a city of Toronto, there has been tension between its closest rival, Montréal. Even before hockey, the two cities

were politically, economically and socially competitive. There is also the natural tension between
the English and French. Add to that the powder
kegs that were the Montréal Forum and Maple
Leaf Gardens during the 1940s, '50s and '60s,
and you have the makings of one of the best
rivalries in hockey to this day.

During the early years of the NHL, both
Montréal and Toronto had difficulty putting
together teams that could win consistently, and
therefore the clubs never really met in the
playoffs (where the hard-core rivalries are born
and bred). But when Conn Smythe took over
control of the Leafs and turned the team into
a competitive organization, Toronto and
Montréal suddenly adopted a quick hatred for
one another.

It was between the 1943–44 season, with the
resurgence of the Canadiens organization and
the arrival of Maurice Richard, and the addition
of general manager Frank Selke in 1946, that
the hatred between Toronto and Montréal really
took off. Selke had been a disciple of Smythe in
Toronto, but after a heated difference of opinion
as to the direction of the Maple Leafs, Selke left
the organization and headed east to become the
general manager of the Montréal Canadiens.

And so, it was during the 1946–47 season that Smythe decided to use a little psychological warfare against his managerial rival in Montréal by saying in the *Globe and Mail* that the Leafs had an interest in acquiring Maurice Richard via a trade. The icing on the cake was an accompanying picture of Richard dressed in a Maple Leafs uniform. Selke, however, was not going to even entertain the idea of trading Québec's hero, and he responded, "Even if you give us the entire Leafs team, and even Maple Leaf Gardens, the answer would still be no!"

This mutual animosity continued and grew throughout the late 1940s and into the '50s, but the Canadiens/Leafs rivalry became legendary in the 1960s when both teams were dominating the regular seasons as well as the playoffs. Apart from the Chicago Blackhawks' Stanley Cup victory in 1961, no other team, other than Toronto or Montréal, won the Cup that decade. And, in 1967, the teams' rivalry culminated in one of the most memorable Stanley Cup finals in hockey history.

It was the last year of the "Original Six," before the NHL expanded into a 12-team league for the 1967–68 season. It also happened to be Canada's centennial year, and Montréal was hosting the 1967 Expo, or World's Fair. The tension between the cities was in the air long before the Stanley Cup series of 1967–68 got underway. The hostility was made that much greater because the majority of the Montréal Canadiens from this time were from Québec, and a large part of the Maple Leafs' roster was from around the Toronto area.

During the playoffs, Montréal had easily dispensed with the New York Rangers in four straight games. The Leafs had also played a hard-fought six-game series against the Blackhawks— and had won—but they came out looking tired and unprepared for the Cup final against Mont-réal. The Maple Leafs' head coach, Punch Imlach, knew that his team of aging veterans, such as Terry Sawchuk and Red Kelly, was going to be in tough against the high-flying Canadiens, and Toronto would have a better chance at winning if they played cautiously with a defensive style of game. Imlach's strategy, however, fell apart completely as the Canadiens walked all over the Maple Leafs, winning the opening game 6–2. Luckily, Imlach had a bench full of veterans who had been in this position before, and they did not give up after just one loss. In Game 2, Toronto roared back into the series with a 3–0 win.

The turning point came in Game 3. After battling through three periods, the score remained tied up at two apiece. This was hockey like no one had seen in a long time. Both the Canadiens and the Leafs pounded each other physically while the goaltenders at opposite ends of the ice did everything short of standing on their heads to make the saves. The game was anyone's for the taking, and take it the Leafs did. Toronto's Bob Pulford scored the goal of his career in the first overtime period that ended in what some journalists called one of "the most exciting games of all time."

The well-worn, aging and road-weary Leafs team lost the next game by a score of 6–2, but they won the two final games to take the Cup and finish their initially improbable run to victory.

Soon after this series, the rivalry between Toronto and Montréal began to fade because while the Canadiens continued to play excellent hockey throughout the 1970s, the Leafs dropped to the basement of the league and never made it back to the Stanley Cup playoffs. For the Canadiens, though, the 1970s brought in a cast of new players when Henri Richard and Jean Beliveau, and head coach Toe Blake, seeded their places to a younger generation. Players such as Serge Savard, Guy Lapointe, Larry Robinson, Yvan Cournoyer, Guy Lafleur and goaltender Ken Dryden ushered in a new era of success for the Canadiens that brought the franchise six more Stanley Cups. Montréal Canadiens fans could count themselves lucky—from 1940 to 1980, they got to witness some of the greatest hockey ever played. Montréal had dominated the NHL for four decades, but as more and more teams entered the NHL, it became harder for a franchise—any franchise—to sustain its winning ways season after season. For most of the 1980s, the Canadiens were just another team battling for the right to make it to the Stanley Cup playoffs.

It wasn't until the arrival of a young goaltender from Sainte-Foy, Québec, that the Canadiens returned as a top-tier team in the league. With Patrick Roy in net, Montréal won the Stanley Cup in 1986 and again in 1993.

Since that Cup win in 1993, the Canadiens have moved out of their historic Montréal Forum and into the Bell Centre. The team has had a few good seasons in its new home, but it has failed to make it back into the Stanley Cup finals in the new millennium. There was a brief glimmer of hope at the end of the 2009–10 season when the eighth-place-overall Canadiens defeated the first-place Washington Capitals in the first round, and then defeated the Pittsburgh Penguins, thanks to some excellent work on defence by Josh

Gorges and Hal Gill, and show-stopping goal-tending by Jaroslav Halak. But it was all for naught when the Canadiens met the Philadelphia Flyers in the Eastern final and were eliminated from Stanley Cup contention in five games. Montréal fans are made of hardy stuff, however, and they continue to stick with their team in the blind hope that the Canadiens will one day bring back the years of Les Glorieux.

## The Toronto Maple Leafs
### The Blueshirts, the Arenas and the St. Pats

Toronto has been at the centre of hockey's development since its beginnings in Canada. But from the late 1880s, up until the formation of the National Hockey Association in 1909, Toronto didn't have a team it could call a champion. There were several athletic clubs across the city that iced competitive teams, but they never seemed to gain any ground against their powerful counterparts in Ottawa and Montréal. It wasn't until the arrival of the Toronto Blueshirts in 1912 that the city's hockey fans finally witnessed a quality team. The Blueshirts had almost immediate success as part of the NHA, finishing the 1913–14 season near the top of the league and going all the way to the Stanley Cup final where they beat the Montréal Canadiens to win the franchise's first Stanley Cup.

During World War I, however, it was difficult for teams to find players with enough skill come game time. To make matters worse in Toronto, team owner Frank Robinson joined the military and left the team without a leader. This is when Eddie Livingstone stepped in. Livingstone was a shrewd businessman and could see a good deal a mile away. In 1915, he purchased the Toronto Blueshirts from Robinson and set about building his team, which was not an easy task because many of the players had left Toronto after Robinson quit. With the promise of more money, the rival PCHA had persuaded a good chunk of the Blueshirts to abandon the NHA, leaving Livingstone with the prospect of not having a team to put on the ice when the 1915–16 season began. But Livingstone also owned another Toronto NHA franchise named the Shamrocks. He simply transferred the players from the Shamrocks to the Blueshirts and folded the former. The ease with which Livingstone always seemed to get by rubbed other team owners the wrong way, and he was not left without enemies. One classic example is when, in 1917, after trade disputes and arguments over how the Stanley Cup playoffs should be structured, the owners of the Montréal Canadiens, Québec Bulldogs, Montréal Wanderers and

Ottawa Senators got together and began their plot to get rid of Livingstone.

## Hard Road to the NHL

For the 1916–17 season, the NHA added another Toronto team made up of soldiers from the Canadian military's 228th Battalion. The team was extremely popular with Toronto crowds, but its future in the league was uncertain, given that the team could be called to active duty at any moment and be shipped off to the war in Europe. The 228th Battalion team, however, actually managed to finish the first half of the season in a respectable second place. But the need for soldiers in the war effort grew too great for the military to allow the battalion to continue playing, and the team had to leave halfway through its first season. The owners of the rest of the teams left behind met to decide how to proceed with the remainder of the season. And so it was rather unceremoniously, without any warning or compensation, that they took advantage of the opportunity to dump Livingstone and the Toronto Blueshirts from the NHA. Livingstone immediately sought legal action against the league, but the owners were resolute in their decision to oust him from their operations.

Livingstone tried in vain to get his team back into the NHA, but the owners had blocked all the legal loopholes. To permanently remove any possibility of Livingstone ever getting his foot back in the league, the owners met again in November 1917 and decided to form a new league. The Québec Bulldogs couldn't pull enough players together to form a team in time and were forced to remove themselves from the formation of the league, so this left three teams, two from Montréal and one from Ottawa. If the new league was going to survive as a proper representative of Eastern Canadian hockey, it needed more than two cities within its ranks. With Livingstone on the outside, trying desperately to get back in, it was decided Toronto needed a team completely separate from him in order to secure the new league's success.

On November 26, 1917, all interested parties finally came to an agreement, the new National Hockey League (NHL) was formed and Frank Calder, former NHA secretary-treasurer, was named as the NHL's first president. The NHL had four teams with which to begin operations: two Montréal teams, Ottawa and the new Toronto franchise the league had forced into existence, which was being helmed by a group of approved Toronto businessmen from the Toronto Arena Company. All the players from the Blueshirts were assigned to the new team, and Calder gave Livingstone the order to sell his team to the Toronto Arena Company. Livingstone refused, and so without an official name, the Toronto press

> **QUICK FACT:** For the Torontos' first year of existence, they wore a blue jersey with a large white "T" stitched on the chest.

simply continued to call the team the Blueshirts, or the Torontos. But despite the battle that was going on behind the scenes, the new Toronto team still managed to sign its players and hire its first coach, Dick Carroll. The team that eventually came to be known as the Toronto Maple Leafs officially began operations on December 19, 1917. The team played all their games at the Toronto Arena Company's building, Arena Gardens (also known as Mutual Street Arena).

Losing their first game against the Montréal Wanderers by a score of 10–9, the Torontos got off to a bad start, but the team soon found its chemistry on the ice, and despite the opening loss, finished the season first overall, just ahead of the Montréal Canadiens. For Toronto's first playoff in franchise history, there was not a more fitting opponent than the Canadiens. The eventual rivalry between the two teams began in a two-game total-goal series, the winner of which was to go on to face the PCHA champion for the Stanley Cup.

The home-at-home series began in Toronto in front of a crowd that witnessed the Canadiens lose a brutal game, 7–3. In Game 2, Montréal managed to win 4–3, but since this was a total-goal series, Toronto had the edge with a 10–7 overall score that was good for the win. In just their first year, with all the legal drama continually surrounding the team, the Torontos had managed to make it to the Stanley Cup final against the PCHA champion Vancouver Millionaires.

This best-of-five series went the complete distance, with Toronto eking out a 2–1 victory in Game 5 to win not only the first Cup for their city but also the first Stanley Cup in NHL history. Alf Skinner was the standout player for Toronto, scoring 8 goals in five games, while Toronto's goaltender Hap Holmes was the star in shutting down the Millionaires' offence.

After the victory, however, Toronto didn't have its name engraved on the Cup, as is the custom, because the battle with Livingstone over the team's franchise rights was still ongoing. It was only just before the start of the 1918–19 season that the team was finally (and officially) awarded a franchise and given the name the Toronto Arenas. For years, the space on the Cup for the winners of the 1917–18 Stanley Cup was left blank—it wasn't until 1947 that the NHL engraved the name of the Toronto Arenas into that spot.

Ready for a fresh start at the beginning of the 1918–19 season, the Toronto Arenas came back with many of the same players, save for goaltender Holmes, who was lured west to join the PCHA's Seattle Metropolitans. As it turned out, without their stellar goalie, the Toronto Arenas were unable to beat teams like the Montréal Canadiens or the Ottawa Senators, and the Arenas finished last in the league and out of the playoffs.

Because of these dismal results, the club saw its ticket revenue drop drastically from its debut year only one season earlier. In the off-season, however, the legal wrangling with Livingstone finally ended, with the Toronto franchise sold to a group of Toronto businessmen. To re-energize the fans and players, the owners decided a name change was the ticket to getting things back on track. At this time in Toronto, the Irish made up a considerable portion of the city's population, so to get them out to games, the team was renamed the Toronto St. Patricks, or the St. Pats, for short.

Under new management and a new name, the Toronto St. Pats improved their record for the 1919–20 season, as well as regained a sizable following. But it wasn't until the arrival of the great Cecil "Babe" Dye during the 1920–21 season that things really started to turn around. In addition to his incredible skills on the ice, Dye also played football and minor-league baseball throughout most of his hockey career. He was particularly adept at baseball, which earned him the nickname "Babe," after baseball legend Babe Ruth. Dye's talents on the baseball field were so sought after that in 1921, he was offered the incredible salary of $25,000 (a huge sum in the 1920s) to join the Philadelphia Athletics. When asked where he got his athletic ability, Dye credited his mother, saying, "She knew more about hockey than I ever did, and she could throw a baseball right out of the park." Despite the high salary offer, Dye turned down a pro career in baseball and focused on hockey as his true passion—and besides, he was having way too much fun leading the St. Pats to the top of the league in the 1921–22 season.

In his first season with the St. Pats, Dye led the league with 35 goals and then continued his outstanding play into the 1921–22 season. Toronto finished the regular season just three points behind the Ottawa Senators and went on to meet its provincial rival in the NHL finals for the second year in a row. Ottawa had handed the St. Pats a beating in the 1921 NHL finals, winning the two-game total-goal series by a final score of 7–0. But this time around, the St. Pats had goaltender John Ross Roach, whose acrobatic style and lightning-fast reflexes helped the St. Pats beat the Senators 5–4 in, again, a two-game total-goal series.

Up next for the Toronto St. Pats were the Vancouver Millionaires, in Ontario for the Stanley Cup finals. Toronto looked tentative in the opening game, losing 4–3, but a 2–1 win in overtime in Game 2 re-energized the club. They lost Game 3, but Dye put in an incredible performance in the final two games of the series. He scored four of Toronto's five goals in a 5–1 win to take the Stanley Cup. In total, Dye scored 9 of 16 Toronto goals in the five-game series. Goalie Roach also recorded the first shutout by an NHL rookie, in Game 4 with a 6–0 win. After only five years in the NHL, Toronto had two Stanley Cups under its belt, but more importantly, the team had developed a huge—and loyal—fan following.

**QUICK FACT:** Game 2 of the 1921–22 NHL finals was the last time an NHL game was played on natural ice. The St. Pats and the Senators played the second game of their series skating through huge puddles on the natural ice surface in Ottawa's Dey's Skating Rink.

Over the next few years, more and more teams entered the NHL, and competition for

Lord Stanley's Mug intensified. St. Pats veterans such as Reg Noble and Jack Adams could no longer provide the punch that was needed on the ice, and the team's fortunes sank into the basement of the league. By the start of the 1926–27 season, the group that owned the St. Pats was considering selling the team.

## The Arrival of Conn Smythe

Meanwhile, in the ever-expanding NHL, the New York Rangers were busy assembling a team for their inaugural 1926–27 season. Of all the players available, Toronto's Babe Dye was the man that every team wanted to add to its lineup. He was hockey's biggest star and was a welcome addition to any franchise—new or old. Rangers general manager Conn Smythe, on the other hand, didn't think the veteran player had many good years left in his skates and passed on picking him up. Rangers owner Colonel John S. Hammond was so angry that he fired Smythe and replaced him with Lester Patrick. Out one general manager's job, Smythe returned home to Canada and convinced the Toronto owners to sell him the St. Pats for $160,000. In February 1927, what turned out to be one of the most important deals in Toronto hockey history occurred, as the keys to the Mutual Street Arena and Toronto St. Pats club were transferred over to Smythe.

Not wasting any time making his mark, Smythe renamed his team the Toronto Maple Leafs (after the World War I Canadian Maple Leaf regiment) on February 15, 1927, and changed the team's uniform to the iconic blue-and-white jersey with the maple leaf crest. In their first game as the Maple Leafs on February 17, 1927, Toronto won 4–1 over the New York Americans.

But the new management, new name and new jersey weren't enough to improve the Leafs' standings, and Toronto remained at the bottom of the NHL over the next two seasons. Smythe, however, was committed to seeing his franchise succeed. Irvine "Ace" Bailey was slowly yet surely emerging as the team's leader, the head coaching job was handed over to the stern yet brilliant Dick Irvin and goaltender Lorne Chabot was more than reliable. It was the further addition of three players who came to be known as the "Kid Line," however, that brought the Toronto Maple Leafs back to a Stanley Cup final.

Charlie Conacher, Joe Primeau and Busher Jackson made their full-season debut during the 1929–30 season, and by the following year, they had helped change the direction of the franchise. These three players brought to the ice a fast-paced, high-scoring game that Toronto fans had not seen since a few years before when Babe Dye was the top scorer on the team. Toronto's Mutual Street Arena was packed to the rafters for every home game, when just two years earlier the arena could barely give its tickets away. At this rate, Smythe realized that if the Leafs were going to be a premier team, they would need a top-notch facility.

Prior to the start of the 1931–32 season, Smythe baught a plot of land on the corner of Carlton, Wood and Church streets, and construction began on the Leafs' new arena. On November 12, 1931, the Toronto Maple Leafs played their first game in Maple Leaf Gardens before a crowd of 14,000 fans. Unfortunately, they lost the inaugural game to the Chicago Blackhawks by a score of 2–1, but this was a season that was going to get a lot better for Leafs fans.

The line of Jackson, Conacher and Primeau could not be stopped, and the defence of Hap Day and King Clancy was shutting down opposing offences left and right. The Leafs finished third overall in the standings and faced off against the Blackhawks in the opening round of the playoffs in a two-game total-goal series.

The first game was a boring, defensive affair that the Hawks took 1–0, but the Kid Line couldn't be contained forever and opened up on the Chicago club with a 6–1 win in the second game to take the series 6–2. The Leafs then faced the Montréal Maroons in a playoff semifinal that turned out to be a physical series in which the youth of the Leafs prevailed. The Toronto Maple Leafs beat out Montréal and found themselves in their first Stanley Cup final against the New York Rangers.

The Rangers had finished the regular season with more points than the Leafs and had enjoyed a week off before the start of the Stanley Cup finals, but New York was shaky in the opening game of the series. Former Leafs goaltender John Ross Roach looked unsteady before the home crowd of about 16,000 screaming Rangers fans. The job of each team's goaltender, however, was made all the more difficult because that first game was rife with penalties. Over 20 penalties were dealt out to the teams by the time the clock ran out. But when all the smoke cleared, the Leafs were the victors, with a 6–4 win. Jackson was the star for Toronto, scoring a hat trick.

Game 2 was scheduled to be played in Madison Square Garden, but because of a scheduling conflict with a circus, the Stanley Cup playoffs had to be moved to Boston Gardens, where the Rangers quickly secured themselves a two-goal lead. New York completely fell apart later in the game, though, when Clancy and Conacher potted two goals each. The game ended 6–2, Leafs, and the Rangers were on the verge of losing their chance at winning the Cup in the best-of-five series. Back in Toronto in front of the hometown fans for Game 3, the Leafs were confident they could end the series.

In front of a capacity crowd of 14,366 at Maple Leaf Gardens, the Leafs played a great game. They controlled almost every period, despite the hat trick by Rangers forward Frank Boucher, and Roach's performance in net made the difference in the game, as he looked like a nervous rookie in the Rangers' goal, letting in easy shots. When the final buzzer sounded, Toronto had won the game by a final score of 6–4 and had in their possession their first Stanley Cup as the Maple Leafs. They didn't win another Cup until 1942, but the Leafs still managed to stay near the top of the league while energizing the fan base and ingraining the Leafs brand into the fabric of the city.

## The Original Six Years

When the Ottawa Senators folded operations in 1934 and the Montréal Maroons closed their locker-room doors in 1938, Canadians were left with just two teams to cheer for, either the Montréal Canadiens or the Toronto Maple Leafs.

It was a choice that ruined friendships and tore households apart. This was the era of the Original Six, when Toronto and Montréal were among the best teams in the NHL and Canadian hockey was at its highest peak to date. During this period, the Toronto Maple Leafs accomplished some of the greatest feats in not just franchise history but in the history of the game. It all started with the 1942 Stanley Cup final versus the Detroit Red Wings.

With a solid lineup of new faces for the start of the 1941–42 season, players such as Sweeney Schriner, Syl Apps and Turk Broda had the Leafs once again looking like a team that could go far into the playoffs. The team was void of superstars, per se, but coach Hap Day had built up a good team system that was followed to the letter and that worked for the players. Toronto finished out the season second place overall and went into the semifinals against the league-leading New York Rangers.

Toronto opened up the series with a win at home and never looked back. Yes, the games were close, but Broda kept the Leafs in the series, and in six games, Toronto found itself in the Stanley Cup final against the Detroit Red Wings.

The Leafs weren't all that disappointed to have the Red Wings as their opponents. Detroit had finished the regular season with a less-than-stellar record of 19–25–4, and the team was worn out from two physical series against the Montréal Canadiens and Boston Bruins. Detroit had a decent forward line with reliable goal scorers and set-up men such as Sid Abel, Don Grosso and Syd Howe, but their defence and goaltender Johnny Mowers had struggled all season, making the Red Wings the favourites to bow out of the finals early. Gambling establishments, aware of the Red Wings' shortcomings, gave the Leafs 8–5 odds of winning the Cup. But, fully aware of his team's problems, Detroit coach Jack Adams knew his Red Wings had one thing he believed the Leafs did not. "We may not have the greatest hockey club in the world, but it's a club that's loaded with fighting heart. If there's anything that wins hockey championships, it's just that," said Adams.

In hindsight, Adams' words seemed prophetic, as the Red Wings hammered the Leafs into submission. Detroit won all three of the best-of-seven series' first games and was poised to sweep its way to the Cup. It was do or die for the Leafs, and before the start of Game 4, the players in the Toronto dressing room knew the task ahead of them was monumental. Said Syl Apps in an interview in Jack Batten's book *The Leafs:*

> *I remember sitting in that dressing room, waiting for the fourth game to start. The only thing on our minds was, we can't go back to Toronto if we lose this game too. We were thinking we couldn't lose four straight and face the people back home.*

What the Leafs were asking for was a miracle. In the history of team sport, coming back from a 3–0 deficit in the finals of a playoff is extremely rare. And yet, a miracle is what they got. The Leafs squeaked by with a 4–3 win and won the next three games to take the Stanley Cup. This was the only time in history that a team had come back from 3–0 in the Cup finals.

Toronto won another Cup in 1945, and led by the brilliance of forward Ted Kennedy, the Leafs became the first team in NHL history to win three Stanley Cups in a row, taking the prize from 1947–49 and again in 1951. These were some of the best years for Leafs Nation—the rivalry with

**QUICK FACT:** The only other teams to later claw their way back from a 3–0 deficit in the playoffs were the 1975 New York Islanders against the Pittsburgh Penguins in the quarter-finals, and the Philadelphia Flyers against the Boston Bruins in the conference semifinals in 2010.

Montréal was at its peak and, in addition to Kennedy, Toronto had players such as Howie Meeker and Max Bentley who electrified the crowds nightly. Then there was Bill Barilko, arguably one of the most famous Toronto Maple Leafs ever. Barilko was the hometown hero who scored the Stanley Cup–winning goal in overtime that beat out the Montréal Canadiens in the 1951 finals. A week after the massive celebrations died down, Barilko and a friend decided to get away from the city and head up north on a fishing trip. They never reached their destination, and it wasn't until 11 years later in 1962 that someone spotted the wreckage of Barilko's small plane. Because of his overtime game-winner, his mysterious disappearance immediately afterward and the Leafs' 11-year Cup drought until his body was found, Barilko's story has become the stuff that myths are made of. The band The Tragically Hip actually immortalized Barilko's story in their 1992 hit song "Fifty-Misson Cap," bringing the young Leafs defenceman's story to a whole new audience.

## The Greatest Leafs Generation

After their Cup win in 1951, the Toronto Maple Leafs watched the Detroit Red Wings and Montréal Canadiens dominate the new era of the Original Six. It was a tough position to be in because the

Leafs had a solid young lineup that included George Armstrong, Dave Keon, Tim Horton and the phenom Frank Mahovlich. Conn Smythe had faith in his new coach Punch Imlach, however, and in 1962, the Toronto Maple Leafs that had electrified Toronto in the 1940s returned. The team moved away from a tight defensive system and opened the game up to offensive-minded players like Mahovlich and Keon. These players could score, but they could also hit and had tough guys like Horton and Bob Baun to protect the defensive lines. It was Canadian-style hockey at its best, and the team claimed the 1962 Stanley Cup championship, thanks in no small part to Imlach's coaching methods. His style of hockey was simple, based on hard work and hockey fundamentals, and it led to two more Cups in 1963 and 1964.

The 1964 playoff win against the Detroit Red Wings was a memorable one for the Leafs because not only was it the second time the franchise won three consecutive Stanley Cups, it was also the series that produced a moment in hockey history that has come to exemplify what it means to play Canadian hockey. It all happened in Game 6 when a powerful shot from Gordie Howe found its way into the tiny unprotected area of Leafs defenceman Bob Baun's leg. "I heard a boom like a cannon," Baun said. "It was the bone cracking."

Like a true warrior, Baun tried to stay in the game and stop the Red Wings' advance, but the pain was too much to bear, and he collapsed on the ice. He was carried off on a stretcher, and doctors wanted to have him transported to hospital for x-rays, but Baun refused to leave his team and ordered the doctors to freeze his leg as the Leafs headed into overtime. The doctors complied, and surprising everyone in the arena, Baun took his place on the Leafs' bench, jumping out on his line change despite the pain radiating up his leg. The Leafs carried the puck into the Red Wings' zone, then dropped it back to Baun, who took a lazy shot on goaltender Terry Sawchuk. The puck deflected off a player, fooling Sawchuk, and went straight into the back of the net. Baun had scored the Game 6 overtime winner to keep the Leafs in the series—and on a broken leg, no less! Somehow he played again in Game 7 and helped the Leafs win their third straight Cup. "I guess it was my pain tolerance and the mental ability to block things out," said Baun.

## The Final Cup

It was a remarkable finish for the Leafs, but the team began to show its age soon afterward.

The stars that had brought Toronto the Cup three consecutive times in the early 1960s were starting to slow down considerably by the time the 1966–67 season rolled around. Guys like Baun, Sawchuk, Red Kelly and Tim Horton were a season or two away from retirement, and goaltender Johnny Bower looked older than his years. No one expected the team to make it into the playoffs that year, let alone the Stanley Cup final. But the Leafs' Cinderella story wasn't over yet. Toronto battled the powerful Canadiens in the final and beat all the odds to win the Maple Leafs' 13th Cup. Few fans or sportswriters at that time would have predicted that more than 40 years later, Toronto was still going to be waiting for another Cup.

Since 1967, the Toronto Maple Leafs have experienced a series of few highs and many lows. Harold Ballard, owner, general manager and dictator of the Leafs from 1972 until his death in 1990, plagued the team with bad trades and horrible draft choices, and the team had a terrible unlucky streak in their playoff draws that saw them meet the strongest teams in the early rounds. The 1970s and 1980s were not happy times for Leafs fans. Even the 1990s were questionable, with the brightest spot coming in the 1992–93 season. Doug Gilmour and the brilliance of goaltender Felix Potvin took the Leafs to within a hair of making it into the Stanley

Cup finals for the first time since 1967, and the series would have been against the Canadiens, had the Leafs not run into Wayne Gretzky at the helm of a determined Los Angeles Kings team that ended up eliminating the Leafs. Fans are religiously dedicated to the boys in blue, however, and they are the ones who keep the hope alive that one day the Cup will return to Toronto.

# Chapter 8

# Canadian Hockey's First Shrines

## The Montréal Forum

When construction of the Montréal Forum began in the 1920s, it was not to house the Montréal Canadiens. The legendary building on the corner of Ste-Catherine Street and Atwater was originally built for Montréal's newest franchise, the Maroons. But the Canadiens were proving to be the bigger draw in town, and since their home in the Jubilee Arena was too small to accommodate their growing number of fans, it was decided the Canadiens would share the Forum with the Maroons. The new arena was big and had plenty of room to accommodate fans—it was perfect.

So share the teams did, and between 1924 and 1938, the Montréal Forum was home to both the Canadiens and the Maroons. During that time, the Forum was the site of some of the most intense matchups between the two Montréal teams. With francophone Montréal cheering for the Canadiens, and anglophone Montréal cheering for the Maroons, the Forum was always full of excitement, emotion and violence, both on the ice and off. Police were regular visitors to the Forum and usually had to break up the fights in the stands. The Maroons fell on hard times in the late 1930s, however, and were forced to fold at the end of the 1938 season. This left the Forum all to the Habs.

The Montréal Forum, one of the most recognized and most celebrated temples of hockey in NHL history, saw the Montréal Canadiens through 22 of their 24 Stanley Cups, witnessed the performances of some of the team's greatest stars and was the site of more than a few of the most important moments in the history of the city.

In its 70 years of existence, the Forum underwent major renovations in 1949 and again in 1968 to accommodate ever-increasing crowds and to bring in more revenue. But it wasn't enough as the Canadiens organization continued to expand, and "bigger and better" became the words of the day. The Canadiens were forced to start looking for a new site to call home because it was just too expensive to undertake another major reno of the old Forum. As the Canadiens' future home, team president Ronald Corey chose an empty lot in the downtown area, near all the modern amenities people had come to expect. Today, the old Montréal Forum is home to a Future Shop, a gym, a movie theatre complex and a host of other little stores, and Canadiens fans keep hoping that the team can bring the glory and the prestige of the Forum back to their new home at the Bell Centre.

## Maple Leaf Gardens

With two Stanley Cups under their belt since joining the NHL nine years earlier, by 1926 the Toronto St. Patricks were one of biggest draws in town. There was just one problem with the demand for tickets; the Mutual Street Arena, or Arena Gardens, as it was more commonly called, that had been the home of Toronto's NHL team since 1917, had seen better days and couldn't fit the growing number of fans in its seats. Conn Smythe knew another arena had to be built in order for the Leafs to survive, and he envisioned a grand hockey palace that was to be the envy of all the other teams in the league. A few obstacles stood in Smythe's way, however.

As early as Smythe's purchase in 1927 of the Toronto franchise, he had imaginings of a new arena for his team. And with the team's success on the ice, his confidence in moving ahead with his decision soared. Smythe started to secure the necessary financial support he needed and, by 1930, began the difficult task of finding the perfect location. Several sites were considered, including one at the corner of Yonge and Fleet streets, but the final spot chosen was a lot bounded by Carlton, Wood and Church streets. The same architectural firm that designed Toronto's Union Station was selected to build the new arena, and on June 1, 1931, construction began on Maple Leaf Gardens. Smythe wanted the building ready for the opening game of the 1931–32 season and pushed the construction crew to finish the arena as quickly as possible. The paint had barely dried when, just 166 days later, on November 12, 1931, Maple Leaf Gardens was open to host its first NHL game.

Maple Leaf Gardens has seen some of the most incredible moments in hockey history. For example, it was on Maple Leaf ice that the NHL had its first All-Star game on February 14, 1934, as a benefit for injured Toronto star Ace Bailey to help him pay his bills and take care of his family. The Maple Leafs defeated the NHL All-Stars by a score of 7–3, and at the end of the game, Bailey's famous number 6 jersey was the first jersey in NHL history to be retired. The good times continued through to the 1970s, when the team's glory days finally appeared to be over. Toronto's fortunes didn't change in the 1980s, and it wasn't until the early 1990s that things started to turn around again. It was thus decided a new home was needed to welcome in the newest era of the Toronto Maple Leafs. Construction began, and on February 13, 1999, the Maple Leafs played their final game under the Gardens lights in a 6–2 loss to the Chicago Blackhawks, and Doug Gilmour scored the final goal in Gardens history. The Toronto Maple Leafs now play their games at the Air Canada Centre, where the hope still lives on that a Stanley Cup banner will one day be raised again in the rafters.

# Chapter 9

# Hockey Moves South

There's no doubt that Canada is the home of hockey and will always be considered as such, but you can't look back at the history of the game and not acknowledge the role the U.S. has played in hockey's development as an international phenomenon.

## Hockey's First American Star

*He was an ideal worthy of everything in my enthusiastic admiration, yet consummated and expressed in a human being who stood within ten feet of me.*

–F. Scott Fitzgerald on Hobey Baker

At a time when hockey was just making its first forays into the U.S. in the late 19th and early 20th century, there arose a player who brought the marginal sport to the attention of the American public with a celebrity that had yet to be experienced south of the border. He was the right kind of athlete who played at the right time. He was the kind of man who could get the sophisticated New York set cheering along with the Average Joes. He was Hobey Baker.

Hobart "Hobey" Amory Hare Baker had a lot of things going for him: he was the captain of the Princeton University football club, he was the star of the school's hockey team, he excelled in his studies and he was well known in the social circles of Manhattan's elite. His strength of character and athleticism even caught the eye of writer F. Scott Fitzgerald, who immortalized the young Baker in his novel, *This Side of Paradise*, depicting him as he lived—a handsome young man with the world in the palm of his hand, a man whom all the ladies wanted and all the men emulated.

Born in the Philadelphia suburb of Bala Cynwyd, Baker first played organized hockey at the elite St. Paul's School in Concord, New Hampshire. He also played on the school's football and baseball teams, but it was hockey that he really loved.

Under the watchful eye of St. Paul's famed hockey coach Malcolm Gordon, Baker learned the nuances of the game and developed into a powerful skater. Gordon had a keen hockey mind, and he was pivotal in formalizing the sport in the U.S. because he was the first person in the country to write down an actual set of rules. He was also instrumental in moulding Baker into the star he was destined to become. Gordon's job was made easy, given that Baker took to the game with such passion. On many a cold winter night, Baker could be found out on the school rink, skating and stickhandling in the dark. By his senior year at St. Paul's, Baker possessed a flair on the ice that became his signature and helped lead his teams to new heights. Without Baker, the St. Paul's hockey team was good, but with him, the team was invincible. Case in point: near the end of his time at St. Paul's, Baker was crucial in handing his future team, the Princeton Tigers, its only loss of the year.

After graduating from St. Paul's, Baker entered Princeton in 1910 and quickly became one of the school's most popular and active students. But because Princeton didn't allow students to participate in more than two varsity sports, Baker dropped baseball and concentrated on football and hockey. Soon, everyone in the halls of the Ivy League school knew the name Hobey Baker. On top of being named Princeton's all-American football captain, Baker was also the star forward on the hockey team. He was the perfect athlete: solid frame, incredible reflexes, hand-eye coordination like no other and courage that came through in every stride. In his first season with the Princeton Tigers hockey club, Baker led his squad through an undefeated season that ended with the intercollegiate championship.

Since hockey was a relatively new sport in the early 20th century, Princeton didn't have an arena of its own, which forced the Tigers to play all their home games at New York City's St. Nicholas Rink. Baker's skill on the ice was already established at Princeton, but after a few games in the big city, his fame skyrocketed there as well.

As a rover, Baker had ultimate freedom on the ice to display his puck-handling and skating prowess. Crowds rose in anticipation when Baker made one of his patented moves, circling around the net one or two times to gain momentum and then speeding toward the opposing goal on a magnificent end-to-end rush. His brilliance on the ice was such an attraction that the St. Nicholas Rink manager often proudly proclaimed on his marquee, in bright, bold letters, "Hobey Baker Plays Here Tonight!" and on those nights Manhattan's social elite came out of their penthouses to wait in lines that stretched around the block. Baker put in such dominant performances during these games that the Princeton Tigers were often called "Baker and Six Other Players."

Baker played simply for the love of the game and was a consummate gentleman on and off the ice, which only served to increase his popularity. If another player on the opposing team was injured, Baker was always the first to his side, and in his entire hockey career he was only penalized once, for slashing, in a game against Princeton's Harvard rivals. Even after almost single-handedly defeating team after team, Baker could be counted on to visit his opponents' locker rooms to offer a handshake and a pat on the back for a game well played. It was not something done out of spite or to rub his victory in the opponents' faces; Baker was, by definition, a true sportsman. This attitude caused him to be loved by his teammates and opponents alike, for he remained unaffected by his celebrity, even as crowds lined up to see him and chanted his name every time he touched the puck. Baker was such a virtuoso of the game that the *Boston Journal* declared him, "the greatest amateur hockey player ever developed in this country or in Canada."

Baker finished out his college hockey years by helping the Princeton Tigers to yet another collegiate title in 1913–14, but because there were no professional leagues in the U.S. at the time of his graduation, Baker took a Wall Street job with J.P. Morgan. He quickly recognized his need for the adrenalin rush of sporting competition—the financial world bored him senseless. To make things worse, executives used Baker as a trophy of sorts, bringing new clients into his office to get a peek at the legendary Hobey Baker, making him feel like a museum piece and providing a constant reminder of his past glory days. To bring some excitement back into his life, Baker joined the St. Nicholas Rink's elite amateur hockey club.

On December 11, 1915, Baker and his new club played the Montréal Stars for the Art Ross Cup (given to the champions of the elite amateur-league circuit). Baker was his usual self on the ice, scoring twice and setting up three goals as his St. Nicholas team easily defeated the Montréal squad. The following day, the defeat was headline news as Montréal papers gave full credit to America's secret weapon: "Uncle Sam has had the cheek to develop a first-class hockey player...We didn't want the St. Nick's to win but Baker cooked our goose so artistically that we enjoyed it."

Lester Patrick, hockey legend and owner of the PCHA, heard of Baker's exploits in the game and tendered an offer of $3500 (a hefty sum in those days) for him to turn pro and move to Canada. Baker didn't think long about the offer, refusing for the simple reason that he only played hockey for fun, and turning pro would remove the exhilaration of the game.

One can only imagine the impact Baker would have had on hockey if he had taken Patrick's offer. Might he have won a Stanley Cup? Would he have eventually joined the NHL? What records would he have set? All questions that have no answer but are interesting to imagine, given Baker's impact on the game as an amateur.

Still beset with the need for the glory and the thrills he achieved in his college years, Baker volunteered to join the air force in April 1918. Not surprisingly, he quickly distinguished himself as one of the best pilots in the sky. Stationed in Ypres, Belgium, just one month after joining the war effort, Baker shot down his first enemy plane in a deadly dogfight and won France's Croix de Guerre for his exceptional valour under fire.

Baker relished every moment, and even though the major air battles of the war had already been fought by the time Baker joined the air force, he is credited with having shot down three enemy planes in his career, just two short of the coveted "ace" status. (Although, because of Baker's celebrity, he is often credited with shooting down more than 10 enemy planes.)

It's not surprising that Baker's squadron, the Lafayette Escadrille, became renowned for the glamour of its officers clubhouse and for the talents of its pilots. Would it be any other way for Baker? Like-minded men surrounded him, and he felt happy in a world that was far removed from the monotony of his Wall Street office.

In describing his experiences during the war, Baker often reverted to the metaphors he knew best, describing the sky as his icefield and saying that he dodged enemies like he did players. But the glory he managed to regain during the war didn't last long when all battles came to an end on November 11, 1918. Unlike most who fought in the war, Baker did not look forward to returning to his desk job in New York, and he pleaded with his military superiors to allow him to remain in France. His request was denied, and he was handed his orders to return to the U.S. immediately.

Due to catch a train to Paris on December 21, 1918, then board a ship back home, Baker went down to the airplane hangar and told one of the ground crew that he wanted to take just "one last flight." The crew member refused Baker's request, stating that no planes were available and the cold, rainy weather wasn't good for the planes' engines. Baker pulled rank and told the other man that he didn't need his permission to test one of the repaired planes.

Baker lifted off into the drizzle and was just a few metres off the ground when he drove the throttle to maximum and pulled into a vertical climb that pushed the plane to its breaking point. He just managed to level off when the engine sputtered out. Baker tried to impose his formidable will on the airplane, but even he couldn't stop it from crashing to the ground. The terrified ground crew rushed over to the wreckage, but they were too late to save Baker, and he died in their arms.

Despite never playing a professional hockey game, Hobey Baker left an indelible mark that reverberates to this day. He played the game with a grace, precision and professionalism that was rare for the time, and still is to this day. He had talents that must have been handed down by the gods, and like so many other young, promising men taken from the world too soon, it seems those gifts came with a heavy price.

Baker left behind a legacy, with various symbols of success that now bear his name. The Hobey Baker Memorial Award (sometimes called the Heisman Trophy of hockey) is awarded annually to the most outstanding American collegiate hockey player. His old Princeton Tigers squad continues to play on the ice of the arena named in his honour, and in 1945, when the Hockey

Hall of Fame opened its doors in Toronto, Baker was one of the first players to receive his spot in the pantheon of hockey's greatest players. He is also a member of the U.S. Hockey Hall of Fame Museum.

## Americans Take the Grail

Canadians have always taken hockey seriously, and they can be fiercely nationalistic when it comes to being the best at the sport, but many years ago, when the Stanley Cup measured only a few centimetres tall, an American squad from Seattle took home the title of the best team in North America. The team to own this distinction is the 1917 Seattle Metropolitans of the PCHA.

Today, the Stanley Cup is the property of the NHL and no other league can play for it, but in the early days of hockey, when the Stanley Cup was still a challenge cup, the top team from both the NHA and PCHA competed for the right to be named champion. And so, at the end of the 1917 season, the Montréal Canadiens won the NHA finals and earned the right to face off against the PCHA champion Seattle Metropolitans. The Canadiens travelled to Seattle to play the Metropolitans in a best-of-five series for the Cup, and this was only the second time since the Cup was first awarded in 1893 that an American-based team was going to play for the championship. (The Portland Rosebuds just one year earlier had lost the Cup finals to the Montréal Canadiens.)

The Canadiens had some legendary players in their lineup in 1917, including forward Didier Pitre, goaltender Georges Vezina and natural goal-scorer Newsy Lalonde, but the Metropolitans were no pushovers, either. Seattle goaltender Harry "Hap" Holmes was a veteran of the professional hockey circuit and had played in the eastern leagues for many years before jumping over to the PCHA, and centre Bernie Morris led his team in scoring that year with 37 goals in 24 games. The series had all the makings of an exciting, high-scoring adventure.

Game 1 on March 17, 1917, was held at the Seattle Ice Arena, near the present-day Olympic Hotel, but things did not go in the Metropolitans' favour. Led by Pitre, who scored 4 goals, the Canadiens walked away with an easy 8–4 victory. The early loss didn't bring Seattle down. In the second game, the Metropolitans hammered the Canadiens 6–1 to tie up the series. The beating in Game 2 seemed to take all the energy out of the Montréal squad, and the Metropolitans walked away with two easy wins in Games 3 and 4 with scores of 4–1 and 9–1, respectively. Holmes was probably the most solid player on the Seattle team, finishing the series with a 2.9 goals-against average, and Morris got the job done in the other end of the rink, scoring 14 of Seattle's 23 series goals.

The Metropolitans disposed of the Canadiens in four games to become the first U.S.-based team to have their names engraved on the Stanley Cup. However, as an interesting side note, all the players on the Metropolitans, save for Everard Carpenter, were born in Canada.

## The NHL Expands into the U.S.

Professional hockey was a part of the northern U.S. for many years, but for a long time, Canadian teams were the only ones that belonged to the NHL. The Ottawa Senators, Québec Bulldogs, Hamilton Tigers, Montréal Wanderers, Montréal Canadiens and Toronto St. Patricks continuously played for the Cup, without any other challengers. Others had tried to break into the league, but the NHL wasn't ready for expansion. In 1923, however, the NHL was, at least, prepared to listen.

At a league meeting, Montréal Canadiens owner Leo Dandurand introduced Tom Duggan to the other owners and league president Frank Calder. Some in the room already knew Duggan as the man who four years earlier had tried to establish another hockey franchise in Montréal.

This time, though, he came to the meeting with a different proposal—he wanted to bring the NHL to the U.S.

At the time, Canadian players and teams were regularly invited south to participate in exhibition matches at major arenas in New York and Boston. The International Hockey League, with teams that operated in Pittsburgh, and Calumet and Houghton, Michigan, was well stocked with Canadian players. Americans were without a doubt developing a taste for Canada's particular brand of hockey. Duggan recognized that it was time for the U.S. to have a permanent spot in the NHL. After hearing his proposal, everyone at the meeting agreed, and negotiations started south of the border.

Behind the NHL decision to expand south was their continuing battle with former NHA Toronto Blueshirts owner Eddie Livingstone—his legal wranglings with Calder and Toronto's other team owners over the dissolution of his Toronto franchise lasted for years. The creation of the NHL itself was a way of excluding Livingstone from owning another team, but after his ouster, he tried again and again to create some sort of competition for his rival. The NHL granted a team to Duggan mainly because the league had heard of Livingstone's latest plans to open up a new league that focused on teams in southern Ontario and the northern U.S. Granting the franchise to Duggan was, in part, a way of blocking Livingstone's aspirations of an American-centred league. The only issue for Duggan was to find a suitable city to house his team. New York, Brooklyn and Boston were the early favourites for his new NHL squad; New York, especially, because of the access to a huge population and the already-available arenas. Boston, however, won out in the end because it already had a firmly established and vibrant hockey culture. In 1924, the Boston Bruins officially joined the ranks of the NHL along with the Montréal Maroons. The NHL wasn't blind, and it saw the potential for further success in the American market. In 1925, the New York Americans joined the league, and in 1926, the NHL added the Chicago Blackhawks, New York Rangers, Detroit Red Wings and Pittsburgh Pirates. The future success of the NHL now went hand-in-hand with the teams in the U.S., and by the start of the 1938–39 season, the Montréal Canadiens and Toronto Maple Leafs were the only Canadian teams left.

From 1942 to 1967, there were just six NHL teams, and they are most commonly called the "Original Six." But in 1967, the league doubled in size and added six more teams, all from the U.S.

**QUICK FACT:** In order to make hockey easier to understand for the American audiences who were unfamiliar with the names of the players, when the New York Americans joined the NHL, they sewed their names on the backs of their jerseys. The Americans were the first team to do this, and the NHL didn't make the practice mandatory until 1978.

These teams were the Philadelphia Flyers, Los Angeles Kings, Minnesota North Stars, Pittsburgh Penguins, Oakland Seals and St. Louis Blues. Since the 1967 expansion to 12 teams, the NHL has now ballooned to 30 teams, with only six of them from Canada. The league began with Canadian teams, and hockey still remains Canada's game, but in order to thrive and bring in increased revenue, the NHL's expansion into the U.S. was essential, and if it had not made the move, the league might not have lasted beyond a few decades.

# Chapter 10

# The Canadian Expansion

From 1938 to 1969, the Montréal Canadiens and Toronto Maple Leafs were the only Canadian representatives in the NHL. From BC to Newfoundland, families divided their hockey loyalties between the two eastern rivals. Of course, professional teams in the West had existed before, with the PCHA, but franchises such as the Stanley Cup–winning Vancouver Millionaires and the Victoria Cougars, Edmonton Eskimos and a host of other teams had long since come and gone. Hockey in Canada thrived anyway, and not just at a professional level. Canadians searching for more of a hockey fix turned to the junior leagues, and this interest, in part, is a good reason why Canada has continued to produce generation after generation of skilled junior players. Their small towns and markets have been the backbone of Canadian hockey, and people have always supported these amateur teams. In 1970, as more

Canadian cities grew large enough to support a modern NHL franchise, the league finally granted Canada another professional team.

## The Vancouver Canucks

Vancouver was no stranger to hockey. In 1912, the city was booming—it had a population of over 100,000, and money was rolling in from its busy ports. The Patrick family, who had amassed a great deal of wealth in the lumber industry during this time, decided the West needed to have its own professional hockey league. Brothers Lester and Frank Patrick had reputations as astute hockey men because they had played in Montréal for teams such as the Wanderers and the Victorias, so there was no question that they knew their way around the system. The pair successfully worked out the formation of the PCHA, and in 1912, the league had its first season.

But because of the West Coast's temperate climate, an artificial ice rink was built—an expensive venture considering there were only eight in the world. The Patricks got it done, however, and Vancouver's west end was suddenly the home of the Denman Arena. From 1912 to 1926, it was the home of the Vancouver Millionaires and, happily, the 1915 Stanley Cup champions. The PCHA didn't last, however, and the Vancouver

Millionaires were absorbed into the Western Hockey League in 1924 and renamed the Vancouver Canucks. From the 1920s to the mid-1960s, the Canucks won a handful of championships and provided the city with a source of pride, but this was no NHL team, and Vancouver craved a higher calibre of hockey.

In 1966, the Vancouver Canucks were sold to a group of local businessmen who began to lay the groundwork for the team's admittance into the NHL. Thus, when the NHL decided to expand from the Original Six, Vancouver was one of the cities that put in a bid to start the 1967–68 season with a new franchise. The NHL turned it down. It wasn't until 1969 that the Canucks' bid was finally accepted and the new Vancouver team was allowed to join the big leagues.

The first decade wasn't easy. The lone bright spot in those dark years was the 1974–75 season when the team finished atop the Smythe Division and earned their first playoff berth. Unfortunately, that first playoff round was against the Montréal Canadiens, who had finished the season with 30 more points than the Canucks and who had three players in the top 20 in league scoring. The Canucks did manage one win in the series, but were out in five games.

While wearing some of the most horrible uniforms in NHL history (remember the yellow, orange and black V-neck jerseys?), the Canucks managed to sneak into the playoffs with a losing record of 30 wins and 33 losses during the 1981–82 season. They were second in their division, so lucky for them, it guaranteed the team a spot in the post-season. Unlike the rest of the league, the Canucks weren't afraid to stock their lineup with European players, and when it came time for the playoffs, the team pulled together and surprised the entire NHL. Players such as Thomas Gradin, Stan Smyl, Ivan Boldirev, Ivan Hlinka and Lars Lindgren formed the backbone of this 1981–82 team, while Dave "Tiger" Williams was their fist. The Canucks might not have had Wayne Gretzky or Mike Bossy, but they played solid hockey led by the brilliant coaching of Roger Neilson. And so, in the playoffs, Vancouver managed to sweep past the Calgary Flames, Los Angeles Kings and Chicago Blackhawks to make it into the franchise's first Stanley Cup final. Unfortunately, it was against the powerful, high-scoring, tough New York Islanders, and the Canucks couldn't do anything to beat them. They were swept in four games straight.

Over the next several seasons in the NHL, Canucks fans established a deep rivalry with Edmonton and Calgary because it seemed like every year Vancouver made it into the playoffs, they were greeted by either the Oilers or the Flames and promptly eliminated in the first round. And when Gretzky moved from Edmonton to Los Angeles, he still continued to frustrate Canucks fans, eliminating Vancouver from Cup contention on more than one occasion.

Finally, in the 1994 playoffs, the Vancouver Canucks shook off all their competitors to make it to the Stanley Cup final for the second time. On May 31, 1994, the Canucks, led by Trevor Linden and Pavel Bure, faced off against the New York Rangers at Madison Square Garden. Sure, Vancouver had put aside a disappointing season to reach the finals, but the Rangers were also hungry, ready to battle the demons of a 54-year Cup drought. The Canucks jumped out to a 3–1 series lead and were ready to bring the Cup to Vancouver for the first time since 1915, but the Rangers rallied and handed the Canucks a loss that was difficult to swallow. Vancouver fans were, to be blunt, angry. They rioted on the streets of their city, and by the time order was restored, 200 people were arrested, damage was estimated in the millions, and a 19-year-old man was in hospital on life-support after being shot in the head with a rubber bullet.

Since then, the Vancouver Canucks have had a few successes and seen some amazing players go through their lineup. Players such as Bure, Linden, Mark Messier, Markus Naslund, Ed Jovanovski, Cliff Ronning and, more recently, Roberto Luongo and Henrik and Daniel Sedin have all donned a Vancouver jersey. Only time will tell if the team has what it takes to ever bring the Cup back to Vancouver.

## Edmonton Oilers

Before the Edmonton Oilers were an NHL team, they were part of the World Hockey Association (WHA). The WHA dissolved in 1979, however, so the Oilers joined the NHL, creating visions of Cup dreams in the heads of Edmonton fans everywhere.

The Oilers entered the NHL along with the Winnipeg Jets and the Québec Nordiques, but Edmonton was lucky and largely avoided any growing pains, thanks to Wayne Gretzky and the savvy managing of Glen Sather. But while Gretzky tore up the scoresheet, the team as a whole took several years before it truly became competitive in the playoffs. The Oilers' inexperience showed in the 1982–83 playoff finals when they were swept by the veteran New York Islanders in four straight games.

However, it was only so long that fate could keep players like Jari Kurri, Mark Messier, Paul Coffey, Kevin Lowe and Grant Fuhr from winning a Stanley Cup. The next year, the Oilers returned with a vengeance and scored 446 goals during the 1983–84 regular season. With that kind of talent, it was next to impossible to keep the team down, and they made it back into the finals in 1984, once more against the New York Islanders. This time the Oilers got their revenge and took home their first Stanley Cup, winning in just five games. The Oilers won a second Cup in 1985 and had the entire league underneath them by the end of the 1985–86 season. The story going into the playoffs that season was: who could stop the Oilers? In 1986, that job was left to the Calgary Flames in the division finals.

After battling each other to a 3–3 series tie, the provincial rivals faced one more game. Late in the third period of Game 7, the score was tied at 2–2 when Oilers fans watched in horror as defenceman Steve Smith banked a shot off Fuhr that went into his own home net. The goal gave Calgary the win, and the Oilers lost their opportunity for three consecutive Stanley Cup wins.

The 1980s continued to be the decade of the Oilers, however, with another Cup win in 1987 and again in 1988. Nothing seemed to go wrong for the Oilers until the summer of 1988 when the unthinkable happened. In a hurried press conference, a sad Wayne Gretzky announced he was traded to the Los Angeles Kings. It was an unbelievable moment because Gretzky was instrumental in leading the Oilers to their fourth Stanley Cup. Things were made worse when the Oilers met Gretzky's Los Angeles Kings in the first round of the 1989 playoffs and were eliminated in seven games. Captain Mark Messier and goaltender Bill Ranford persevered, though, and won the Oilers a fifth Cup in 1990. But since those glory days, fortune has not smiled on the northern Alberta city.

In the 2005–06 season, the Oilers made an improbable run to the Stanley Cup championship, beating out the Detroit Red Wings, San Jose Sharks and Anaheim Ducks to make it into the finals for the first time since 1990. The series against the Carolina Hurricanes went to seven games only to see the Oilers bow out with a 3–1 loss. Since then, the Oilers have not been able to regain their magic, though the addition of young players like Taylor Hall and Jordan Eberle have given the fans a glimmer of hope for the years to come.

# Winnipeg Jets

When the NHL expanded in the 1970s, Vancouver was the only Canadian team lucky enough to receive a franchise. For all the other professional hockey teams in Canada, the WHA was where it was at. The WHA brought pro hockey to Ottawa, Québec City, Winnipeg, Edmonton and Calgary, but when the association folded in 1979, it left behind five empty, hockey-hungry markets. The Winnipeg Jets were one of the best teams in the WHA, with even a few Avco Cup championships to their name. But when the league dissolved and the Jets were incorporated into the NHL, they had to give up their top players to the Expansion Draft, losing the key ingredients that had made them a successful team in the first place. In the Jets' debut year in the NHL in 1979, they were at the bottom of the league for the entire season. In fact, the Jets only got worse, and the following season, the team won just nine games and finished with only 32 points—one of the worst 70-plus-game seasons on record.

One perk about these terrible seasons, however, was that the Jets were able to pick at the top of the pack during the NHL Entry Drafts that followed their dismal years. And so, by the mid-1980s, the Jets had signed a solid lineup of players that included top draft picks Dale Hawerchuk and

Kent Nilsson. Adding grit were players Dave Babych, Randy Carlyle and David Ellett, and just one year after posting one of the worst winning records in NHL history, the Jets finished the 1981–82 season second place in their division and earned their first appearance in the playoffs. The St. Louis Blues eliminated Winnipeg in the first round, but the Jets had experienced a significant turnaround that, at the very least, kept them away from last place. The Jets' Prairie rivals were strong, however, and despite the firepower of Hawerchuk and Paul MacLean, the team spent nearly the entire 1980s under the thumbs of the Edmonton Oilers and the Calgary Flames. Winnipeg was good, but the Oilers and Flames were simply better. The Jets' faithful always hoped that their club would make it to the Stanley Cup finals, but Winnipeg never advanced past the second round of the playoffs during the team's entire history.

As the team's fortunes took a downward turn in the late '80s and early '90s, and the team's losing records and early playoff exits began to mount, the Jets' expenses inconveniently started to rise. They were one of the league's smallest markets, and continuing a franchise in the city guaranteed a loss of money for the team's owners. Unable to compete with the large-market teams and retain quality players, the Jets were forced to fold. It was a devastating blow for the fans in

Winnipeg who had fully embraced their team despite its losing ways. The Winnipeg Jets played their last game on April 28, 1996, in Game 6 of the opening round of the playoffs against the Detroit Red Wings. The Jets lost the game 4–1 and, thus, the series. Norm Maciver scored the final goal in the franchise's history, and after the season was over, the team was moved to Phoenix, where it became the Coyotes.

## Québec Nordiques

For years, the only NHL team that mattered in Québec was the Montréal Canadiens. Hockey, however, was no less popular in Québec City, and in an era of the NHL long forgotten, the city's Québec Bulldogs actually won the 1912 and 1913 Stanley Cups.

It was a long time before the provincial capital saw a professional hockey team again, so when the WHA came along, there were the Québec Aces and, of course, the junior league teams. But an elite level of hockey was still missing, making Québec City a great market with an eager fan base.

From 1972 to 1979, the Québec Nordiques (meaning "Northmen" or "Northerners") of the WHA joined the Aces in the city and played in front of packed crowds at the Colisée de Québec, and even won the WHA Avco Cup in 1977. When the WHA was shut down, the Nordiques were absorbed into the NHL for the start of the 1979–80 season. Unfortunately, however, the team lost many of its best players to the Expansion Draft, and the Nordiques played their debut NHL season in the bottom tier of the league. There was some promise with young rookies Real Cloutier and Michel Goulet, but it was the acquisition of brothers Peter and Anton Stastny that turned the Nordiques into a playoff team in only their second year in the NHL.

Throughout the early 1980s, the Nordiques steadily improved and became a team to watch into the playoffs. By the 1983–84 season, the Nordiques' Peter Stastny and Goulet had finished the season with a points total of 119 and 121, respectively. And then, going into the playoffs, the Nordiques dispensed with the Buffalo Sabres in the first round, after which the Québec team met up with its provincial rivals, the Montréal Canadiens, in a series that went down in history.

Called the Good Friday Massacre, or *La bataille du Vendredi Saint*, on Friday, April 20, 1984, the Montréal Canadiens went into the Forum with a 3–2 series lead on the Nordiques, and the Montréal team was looking to wrap things up in Game 6. The series had so far been brutally physical, and the Nordiques, if they were going to lose, weren't going down without a fight—literally. From the first drop of the puck, the game saw several fights, but all hell broke loose at the end of the second period when both benches cleared for an old-fashioned hockey brawl. The Canadiens' Mario Tremblay smashed Peter Stastny's nose, and Canadien Jean Hamel was knocked unconscious with enough damage to end his career. A total of 252 penalty minutes were handed out because of this one altercation, but they did nothing to help the Nordiques win, as the team eventually lost the game and the series. Thankfully, for fans, Québec got its playoff revenge on Montréal the following season during the 1985 playoffs. The Nordiques beat out the Canadiens and made it into the Conference finals, but they were promptly eliminated by the Philadelphia Flyers.

In the late '80s and early '90s, the Nordiques' fortunes began to sour. Players were getting old, and goaltenders were struggling. The 1989–90 season saw the Nordiques finish with just 12 wins and a whopping 61 losses. But there was still a glimmer of hope. Because of all the bad seasons, Québec had the high draft-choice picks following those years, and the team started to restock its depleted lineup. Joe Sakic, Mats Sundin and Owen Nolan were Nordiques by 1990, and there was excitement that the young, fresh team was soon going to make its way up the standings.

Like the Jets, however, the Nordiques played in too small a market to maintain a profitable franchise. Not even a stellar team performance could save them, and during the 1994–95 season, by which time the Nordiques had reached the top of the league, the team was shut down. It was moved to Denver and renamed the Colorado Avalanche. Then, just one year later, the team that had been constructed in Québec City won the Stanley Cup in 1996, making it even harder for Québec fans to accept their team's departure. Since the Nordiques left, there have been rumours of an NHL return to Québec City, but nothing has ever come to fruition.

## Calgary Flames

When the Atlanta Flames joined the NHL in 1972, it seemed like a strange move for the pro league. Naysayers criticized the location of a team that played in warm weather and in front of a population whose majority had never seen ice, let alone a hockey game. It was predicted that the Atlanta team would fail, and those predictions turned out to be true. The Atlanta Flames were big money losers by the late 1970s, with no bodies in the arena seats and no TV deal, so when an offer from a group of Calgary businessmen came through, the franchise was sold and the Calgary Flames were born.

It was a great start for the Calgary franchise, as the Flames already had a solid lineup of players who had succeeded in the league for several years. Led by top scorer Kent Nilsson, the Calgary Flames made it into the playoffs in their inaugural year (1981), first beating up on the Chicago Blackhawks in three straight games in a best-of-five series, and then the Philadelphia Flyers in an exciting seven-game series that brought the team into the semifinals against the Minnesota North Stars. Unfortunately, the Flames were tired from their seven-game tilt with the Flyers, and they never quite caught up to Minnesota. The Flames made a series of it, posting 3–2 and 3–1 wins on home ice, but the North Stars won it all in six games, eliminating the Flames from the playoffs. The successful first season of the Calgary Flames was a positive sign, however, and from there, things just got better and better for the new Canadian team.

Something stood in the way of the Flames' ultimate success, however, and that something was the Edmonton Oilers. During the 1983 and 1984 playoffs, the Flames were ousted from a Stanley Cup run by their provincial competition, establishing an intense rivalry—called the Battle of Alberta—that still exists between Edmonton and Calgary to this day. But the Flames finally got their revenge during the division finals of the 1986 playoffs. Six full games and 50 minutes had failed to end the deadlocked series between the Oilers and the Flames, and they went into the final minutes of the game with the score tied at 2–2.

At 5:19 in the third period, Oilers fans watched in horror, and Flames fans watched with joy as Oilers defenceman Steve Smith went behind his own net to set up the move to get outside his team's zone. Looking ahead, Smith shot the puck forward, hoping to hit an Edmonton player on the way out. Instead, the puck struck the back of Edmonton goalie Grant Fuhr's skate and trickled into the Edmonton goal. The Flames' bench erupted in celebration. Calgary managed to hold off the Oilers for the remaining minutes of the game, thus eliminating Edmonton's drive for what would have been their third Cup in a row.

After winning their next series with the St. Louis Blues, the Flames went proudly into their first appearance in the Stanley Cup finals against the Montréal Canadiens. The Flames had all the components to win, with Joe Mullen at his peak, goaltender Mike Vernon on a hot streak and Lanny McDonald at the top of his game. But the long series against the Oilers and the Blues had taken its toll on the Flames, and it didn't help matters that they were up against rookie Canadiens goaltender Patrick Roy. To their credit, the

Flames won Game 1, but the Canadiens took the next four in what appeared to be an easy capture of the Stanley Cup. After coming so far, it was a devastating blow for the Flames.

Calgary spent three more years on the playoff sidelines, exiting early to watch the Oilers win two more Cups. Calgary needed a Cup to prove that they, too, could win. That chance finally came in 1989.

After finishing the 1988–89 regular season at the top of the league, the Flames went into the playoffs feeling they could make a complete run to the Cup. And, after a long series in the opening round against the Vancouver Canucks, the Flames breezed through contests with the Los Angeles Kings and the Chicago Blackhawks to make it to the final against a team they were more than familiar with: the Montréal Canadiens. This time around, though, the Flames' defensive superstar, Al MacInnis, was on fire. In combination with the leadership of Doug Gilmour and the passion of Theoren Fleury, MacInnis and his team pushed past the Canadiens in six games to win Calgary's first Stanley Cup. Afterward, the Flames remained in the top tier of the league but couldn't quite cross the threshold into Cup territory again. The late 1990s were a particularly forgettable time to be a Flames fan, as the team missed the playoffs several years in a row and couldn't even win games on a regular basis. Calgary's fans didn't see any hope on the horizon—that is, until Jarome Iginla finally came out of his shell in the 2001–02 season by scoring a league-leading 52 goals, and a relatively unknown goaltender named Miikka Kiprusoff joined the team in 2003–04.

The same year Kiprusoff joined the Flames, the team made it into the playoffs, albeit as underdogs. The Flames continued to surprise everybody by eliminating the Vancouver Canucks, Detroit Red Wings and San Jose Sharks to make it into the Stanley Cup final against the Tampa Bay Lightning. The series went to Game 7, and the Flames lost in the final by one goal. It was a tough pill for the Flames to swallow, as the entire nation had gotten behind them. Since that magical run, the Flames have played inconsistent hockey, missing out on the post-season a few times and making early exits when they did manage to make it that far. Flames fans can only sit back and hope for another chance at the Cup—with better results, of course.

# Chapter 11

# Hockey Timeline

**2000 BC:** The Ancient Egyptians play a game with curved sticks and a ball. Evidence supporting this is found in modern times in drawings on the walls of pyramids and temples.

**1200 BC:** Celtic nomads bring a game called hurling (or hurley) to Ireland, and the sport gets absorbed into local culture and is still played to this day.

**10th century:** Russians play a game that is similar to the English sport of bandy, a precursor to hockey. Modern historians find references to this activity in old, Russian texts, and it is known that the game is still played in Russia today.

**1700s:** The Mi'kmaq participate in a game similar to hockey that's played on the ice of Tuft's Cove, near Dartmouth, Nova Scotia. The game is called *oochamkunutk*, and each team has approximately eight men who carry sticks and chase a small, puck-like object.

**Early 1800s:** Ice hockey as it is now known is first played in either Windsor, Nova Scotia; the Halifax region; Kingston, Ontario; Montréal, Québec; or Deline, Northwest Territories.

**1825:** While wintering at Fort Franklin, British explorer Sir John Franklin writes in a letter to a friend of a game being played on the frozen waters of Great Bear Lake in the Northwest Territories—"the game of hockey played on the ice was the morning's sport."

**1827:** A poem appears in Halifax's *Acadian Magazine*, and two lines read: "Now at ricket with hurlies some dozens of boys/Chase the ball o'er ice, with a deafening noise."

**1843:** Sir Arthur Henry Freeling, a British officer stationed in Kingston, Ontario, writes in his diary in January: "Began to skate this year, improved quickly and had great fun at hockey on the ice."

**1844:** Thomas Chandler Haliburton writes in his fictional work, *The Attaché; or Sam Slick in England*, of the game of "hurley on the long pond on the ice..." The quotation is taken from a character speaking about his life as a boy growing up in Windsor, Nova Scotia, around the late 1790s.

**1860s:** The Mi'kmaq in the Halifax and Dartmouth areas begin selling hockey sticks to supply local demand. The sticks are sold at markets in Halifax and are given the name MicMac hockey sticks.

**1865:** In Dartmouth, Nova Scotia, the Starr Manufacturing Company begins selling the first modern skates in Canada.

**1866:** A Halifax newspaper reports, "Boys… are playing hockey on the ice and occasionally mimicking the mistakes of such among their betters as are not quite at home upon skates."

**1872:** The rubber hockey puck is invented.

**1875:** Halifax's James Creighton suggests that his Montréal friends take up the game of ice hockey, which they play using "Halifax Rules." A public game put together by Creighton and his teammates is played on March 3, 1875, at Montréal's Victoria Skating Rink, and this match is often credited as the first organized game of hockey.

**1877:** Hockey rules are published, for the first time, in the *Montréal Gazette*.

**1886:** The Amateur Hockey Association of Canada is formed, with four teams in Montréal and one in Ottawa.

**1889 or 1890:** The first women's hockey game is played in Ottawa.

**1893:** Lord Stanley of Preston donates a trophy to hockey that is called the Dominion Hockey Challenge Cup. The first champion is the Montréal Hockey Club.

**1896:** The Winnipeg Victorias are the first team from Western Canada to win the Dominion Hockey Challenge Cup, i.e., the Stanley Cup.

**Late 1800s and early 1900s:** North American ice hockey appears in European countries.

**1899:** The hockey net is created.

**1910:** The Montréal Canadiens play their first game before a home crowd of 3000 at the Jubilee Arena against the Cobalt Silver Kings and win 7–6 in overtime. The Canadiens and six other teams make up the newly established National Hockey Association (NHA).

**1911 and 1912:** Teams in Western Canada and the western U.S. form the Pacific Coast Hockey Association (PCHA). The league introduces several innovations: blue lines are added to divide the ice into three zones, forward passing is allowed in the neutral zone and the 60-minute game is divided into three 20-minute periods.

**1912:** The number of players allowed on the ice is generally reduced from seven to six per team, but the PCIIA continues to use the seven-man system.

**1917:** Four NHA teams reorganize to form the National Hockey League (NHL). A new Toronto franchise, the Arenas, is added. The Seattle Metropolitans of the PCHA are the first U.S.-based team to win the Stanley Cup, after the Cup's trustees rule that teams outside Canada can compete for the trophy.

**1920:** An ice hockey tournament is played at the Summer Olympics in Antwerp, Belgium. It is later declared the first World Ice Hockey Championship. Canada wins the tournament.

**1923:** Foster Hewitt calls the first hockey broadcast for radio, an intermediate-level game between teams from Kitchener, Ontario, and Toronto.

**1924:** The Boston Bruins defeat the Montréal Maroons 2–1 in the first NHL game played in the U.S.

**1924:** Hockey debuts at the first Winter Olympic Games in Chamonix, France, and Canada wins the overall competition.

**1926:** The Chicago Blackhawks, Detroit Cougars (later renamed the Red Wings) and New York Rangers join the NHL.

**1928:** The New York Rangers are the first NHL-based American team to win the Stanley Cup. They defeat the Montréal Maroons in a five-game series to win the title.

**1930:** Clint Benedict of the Montréal Maroons is the first NHL goaltender to wear a mask during a game.

**1931:** On the evening of November 12, Toronto's Maple Leaf Gardens opens for the first time as the Leafs host the Chicago Blackhawks. The visiting team wins 2–1.

**1934:** The NHL holds its first All-Star game on February 14 as a benefit for injured Maple Leafs star Ace Bailey.

**1936:** In the first hockey game broadcast from coast to coast in Canada, the New York Americans defeat the Toronto Maple Leafs 3–2.

**1942:** From 1942 to 1967, the NHL consists of the Montréal Canadiens, Toronto Maple Leafs, Detroit Red Wings, Boston Bruins, New York Rangers and Chicago Blackhawks, the teams known as the "Original Six."

**1943:** The Hockey Hall of Fame governing body is established.

**1945:** At the end of the 1944–45 season, Maurice Richard scores his 50th goal in the 50th and last game of the season.

**1949:** The Toronto Maple Leafs are the first NHL team to win the Stanley Cup three years in a row.

**1952:** *Hockey Night in Canada* debuts on television.

**1955:** The Zamboni ice-cleaning machine makes its NHL launch in Montréal.

**1956:** Jean Beliveau is the first hockey player to appear on the cover of *Sports Illustrated*.

**1958:** Willie O'Ree of the Boston Bruins is the first Black player in the NHL.

**1959:** On November 1, Montréal Canadiens goaltender Jacques Plante regularly begins to wear a goalie mask, the first goalie to do so.

**1960:** The Montréal Canadiens win their fifth consecutive Stanley Cup—the only team to ever accomplish this feat.

**1961:** The Hockey Hall of Fame opens its first permanent location in Toronto.

**1963:** The first NHL Entry Draft is held in Montréal. Only 21 players are selected.

**1967:** The NHL doubles in size, adding teams in Pittsburgh, Los Angeles, Minnesota, Oakland, St. Louis and Philadelphia.

**1970:** The Buffalo Sabres and Vancouver Canucks join the NHL.

**1972:** Bobby Hull is hockey's first million-dollar man after he leaves the Chicago Blackhawks and signs a 10-year, $2.75-million contract with the World Hockey Association's (WHA's) Winnipeg Jets.

**1972:** The Summit Series takes place. Canada's best goes up against the Soviet Union's top players, and Canada wins in the final game of the eight-game series on a tie-breaking third-period goal by Paul Henderson. The final score is 6–5, and the series finishes at 4–3–1.

**1976:** Canada defeats Czechoslovakia 5–4 in the final game of the first Canada Cup tournament.

**1979:** The WHA folds, and the Edmonton Oilers, Québec Nordiques, Hartford Whalers and Winnipeg Jets join the NHL.

**1984:** The Pittsburgh Penguins select Mario Lemieux first overall at the 1983 NHL Entry Draft. The Montréal Canadiens select Patrick Roy 51st overall.

**1990:** Canada is the winner of the first International Ice Hockey Federation (IIHF) Women's World Hockey championship.

**1991:** The NHL introduces video review.

**1992:** The Ottawa Senators and Tampa Bay Lightning join the NHL.

**1993:** The Montréal Canadiens win their 24th Stanley Cup, which marks them as the last Canadian team to win the Cup—and the last team to win the Mug with all North American players on its roster.

**1994:** NHL players are locked out for 103 days at the beginning of the 1994–95 season because of a contract dispute with the league. The regular season, which begins January 20, 1995, is the shortest in 53 years.

**1995:** The Québec Nordiques move to Denver and become the Colorado Avalanche.

**1996:** The Winnipeg Jets move to Phoenix, where they are renamed the Coyotes.

**1997:** Craig MacTavish, the last remaining helmet-less player in the NHL, retires.

**1998:** NHL players compete at the Olympics for the first time, and the Czech Republic wins the gold medal by beating Russia in the final.

The U.S. defeats Canada to win the first Olympic gold medal in women's hockey.

**2002:** Canada's men's hockey team wins the gold medal in Olympic action, 50 years to the day after their last gold-medal win. The Canadian women's hockey team defeats the U.S. to win the Olympic gold.

**2004:** On September 15, NHL owners lock out the players, putting the 2004–05 NHL season on hold, pending a new collective bargaining agreement.

**2005:** On February 16, the 2004–05 NHL season is officially cancelled because of the failure to reach a new collective bargaining agreement. On July 13, the 301st day of the lockout, the NHL and NHL Players' Association (NHLPA) announce a tentative agreement, allowing the league to resume play in October. The NHL introduces a series of rule changes for the 2005–06 season, including shootouts to end tie games.

**2007:** The Anaheim Ducks are the first California-based team to win the Stanley Cup.

**2007:** Sidney Crosby of the Pittsburgh Penguins finishes the 2006–07 season with 120 points, making him the youngest player to lead the league scoring sheet in NHL history. He is 19 years, 244 days old.

**2009:** Sidney Crosby is the youngest NHL captain to lead his team to a Stanley Cup when his Penguins defeat the Detroit Red Wings in seven games.

**2010:** After a shaky start, the Canadian men's hockey team defeats the U.S. to win the Olympic gold medal. Before a home crowd, Sidney Crosby makes history by scoring the gold-medal-winning goal in overtime to win 3–2. Nearly 18 million Canadians watch the game on television. The Canadian women's hockey team also wins gold, defeating the U.S. by a score of 2–0.

**2010:** After a 49-year drought, the Chicago Blackhawks win the Stanley Cup by beating the Philadelphia Flyers 4–2 in this best-of-seven series.

# Notes on Sources

Allen, Kevin and Bob Duff. *Without Fear: Hockey's 50 Greatest Goaltenders*. Chicago: Triumph Books, 2002.

Batten, Jack. *The Leafs: An Anecdotal History of the Toronto Maple Leafs*. Toronto: Key Porter Books, 1994.

Beddoes, Dick, Jim Coleman, et al. *Winners: A Century of Canadian Sport*. Toronto: Canadian Press, 1985.

Carrier, Roch. *Our Life With the Rocket: The Maurice Richard Story*. Toronto: Viking Press, 2001.

Coleman, Charles. L. *The Trail of the Stanley Cup*. Sherbrooke: Progressive Publications, 1969.

Diamond, Dan, ed. *Total Hockey*, New York: Total Sports Publishing, 1998.

Finnigan, Joan. *Old Scores, New Goals: The Story of the Ottawa Senators*. Kingston: Quarry Press, 1992.

Goyens, Chrys, et al. *The Montreal Forum: Forever Proud*. Montreal: Les Editions Felix, 1996.

Goyens, Chrys and Allan Turowetz. *Lions in Winter*. Scarborough: Prentice-Hall, 1986.

Howell, Nancy and Maxwell Howell. *Sports and Games in Canadian Life*. Toronto: Macmillan of Canada, 1969.

Hunter, Douglas. *A Breed Apart*. Toronto: Viking Press, 1995.

Leonetti, Mike. *Maple Leaf Legends*. Vancouver: Raincoast Books, 2002.

McFarlane, Brian. *The Best of It Happened in Hockey*. Toronto: Stoddart Publishing, 1997.

Nicholson, Lorna. *Pink Power: The First Women's Hockey World Championship*. Halifax: James Lormier & Company, 2007.

Norton, Wayne. *Women on Ice: The Early Years of Women's Hockey In Western Canada*. Vancouver: Ronsdale Press, 2009.

Podnieks, Andrew. *The Spectacular Sidney Crosby*. Bolton: Fenn Publishing, 2005.

Podnieks, Andrew, et al. *Kings of the Ice: A History of World Hockey*. Richmond Hill: NDE Publishing, 2002.

Richard, Maurice and Stan Fischler. *The Flying Frenchmen: Hockey's Greatest Dynasty*. New York: Hawthorn Books Inc., 1971.

Spencer, David and Barbara Spencer. *The Pocket Hockey Encyclopedia*. Toronto: Pagurian Press, 1976.

Steward, Barbara. *She Shoots...She Scores*. Toronto: Firefly Books, 1998.

Vaughan, Garth. *The Puck Starts Here*. Fredericton: Goose Lane Editions, 1996.

Whitehead, Eric. *A Hockey Legend: Cyclone Taylor*. Markham: Paperjacks Ltd., 1982.

Wong, John Chi-Kit. *Lords of The Rinks*. Toronto: University of Toronto Press, 2005.

Wong, John Chi-Kit, ed. *Coast to Coast*. Toronto: University of Toronto Press, 2009.

## J. Alexander Poulton

J. Alexander Poulton is a writer, photographer and genuine enthusiast of Canada's national pastime. A resident of Montréal all his life, he has developed a healthy passion for hockey ever since he saw his first Montréal Canadiens game. His favourite memory is meeting the legendary hockey player Jean Beliveau, who in 1988 towered over the awestruck youngster.

Poulton earned his BA in English Literature from McGill University and his graduate diploma in Journalism from Concordia University. He has more than 20 books to his credit, including *Canadian Hockey Record Breakers, Greatest Moments in Canadian Hockey,* and *Greatest Games of the Stanley Cup, Canadian Hockey Trivia, Hockey's Hottest Defensemen, The Montréal Canadiens, The Toronto Maple Leafs* and *Sidney Crosby.*